POWER OF A
FOCUSED LIFE

David S. Philemon

Royal Diadem Publishing Inc.

Dedication

To the Almighty God, my Rock, Refuge, and Source of all wisdom and strength. Thank You for Your unwavering love, grace, and the purpose You've placed within me. May this book bring glory to Your name and draw others closer to You.

And to my beloved spiritual parents, Dr. Paul and Dr. Mrs. Becky Paul Enenche, who have faithfully nurtured and guided me in this journey. Your example of unwavering devotion, godly counsel, and compassionate care has been a beacon of light and strength in my life. Thank you for standing as pillars of faith and for your steadfast commitment to the Kingdom.

ACKNOWLEDGMENTS

This book would not have been possible without the unwavering support, dedication, and talent of an extraordinary team. My deepest gratitude goes to each of you for your contributions, insights, and encouragement throughout this journey.

First and foremost, thank you to Rev. Mimi Philemon my dear wife, Rev. Shina Gentry, and and my assistant pastor Rev. Bright Amudoaghan for your incredible effort, encouragement, and belief in this project. Your support has been instrumental in bringing this vision to life.

To the dedicated leaders of Royal Diadem Publishing, Ide Imogie and Kishawna Bailey, I am immensely grateful for your belief in this project from the very beginning and for investing your time and energy into its development. Your creativity, dedication, and expertise have been the backbone of this endeavor.

I am especially grateful to the Royal Diadem Publishing team— Beulah Orogun, Emmanuella Ben-Eboh, Doyinsade Awodele, Kim Matthews, and Shante Gill, for your meticulous attention to detail, refining every page and ensuring that each word reflects our vision.

A heartfelt thank you to my family, friends, and colleagues whose unwavering support and belief in this project gave me the courage and strength to see it through.

Finally, thank you to all the readers and supporters who make this work meaningful. I am humbled and honored to share this journey with each of you.

With all my gratitude,
David Philemon

CONTENTS

INTRODUCTION

Embracing A Focused Life

In today's world, we are surrounded by distractions - our phones, work, social media, and thoughts often pull us in many directions. It's easy to get caught up in everything around us and lose sight of what matters. But God has a different plan for our lives. He calls us to live with focus—a focus that is centered on Him and His purpose for us.

When we live a focused life, we can walk confidently in the path God has laid out for us. God has a specific plan for each of us, and when we stay focused on that plan, we can live with purpose, joy, and peace.

A life of focus isn't just about getting things done or reaching our goals. It's about aligning our hearts with God's will and trusting Him to guide us. When we focus on God, everything else falls into place. Matthew 6:33 reminds us of this: *"But seek first His kingdom and His righteousness, and all these things will be given to you as well."* In other words, when we put God first, He will care for everything else.

Focus is important because it helps us stay on the right path. Just like a runner in a race who keeps their eyes on the finish line, we need to keep our eyes on God. When we focus on Jesus, we can endure challenges and avoid getting sidetracked. Without focus, it's easy to waste time, miss opportunities, and feel overwhelmed by life. But with focus, we can manage our time wisely, make the most of the gifts and talents God has given us, and live each day with a sense of purpose.

When we give our plans and efforts to God, He helps us stay focused and succeed. We live in a world that constantly pulls us in different directions. When we wake up, distractions await us—our phones buzzing with messages, news headlines demanding our attention, and endless tasks on our to-do list. While some of these things are important, many can distract us from the most crucial focus: our relationship with God.

Focus is a choice we make every day. We can let distractions control our lives or choose to focus on God's purpose for us. It's not always easy, but it's worth it. Choosing focus over distraction often requires discipline. It means setting aside time daily to read the Bible, pray, and seek God's direction. It also means being intentional about how we spend our time and energy. Remembering that we don't have to live a focused life alone is essential. God is with us, guiding and strengthening us every step of the way. God promises to help us as we seek to live a life of focus. He will show us the right path and give us the wisdom to stay on track.

When we struggle to focus or feel overwhelmed, we can ask God for help. Living a focused life is about glorifying God. When we live with purpose and focus, we reflect God's goodness and faithfulness to the world. *"Let your light shine before others, that they may see your good deeds and glorify your Father in heaven."* (Matthew 5:16)

By staying focused on God and His purpose for us, we can be a light to others and lead them to Christ. A focused life honors God. It's a life where we use our time, talents, and resources to serve Him and fulfill His plans for us.

As we go through this book, we will explore how to live with focus in different areas of life, from overcoming distractions to building discipline, aligning with God's prophetic instruction, and fulfilling our God-given potential. With God's help, we can live a life that is not only productive but also profoundly fulfilling and aligned with His will.

Living with purpose is about understanding the "why" behind everything we do. It's the difference between going through life's motions and living intentionally, with focus and clarity. A purpose-driven life is guided by a deep sense of meaning, knowing our actions and choices align with God's plan.

This alignment gives us direction, motivation, and fulfillment beyond temporary success or happiness. Our lives have meaning because God has designed a unique plan for each individual. We live with true purpose when we seek to understand and follow this plan.

A purpose-driven life is built on God's Word, living according to His will and seeking His direction. God's purpose stands above our desires and plans. Aligning with His purpose brings peace, direction, and lasting joy.

Knowing our purpose provides clear direction, eliminating uncertainty. Purpose gives us focus, helping us make decisions aligned with God's plan.

Living purposefully motivates us to persevere through challenges, reminding us of our initial reasons and empowering us to overcome obstacles.

A purpose-driven life brings deep fulfillment, pursuing eternal goals rather than temporary pleasures. Living with purpose inspires others, demonstrating God's work in us. Once you've discovered your purpose, surrender your plans and desires daily to God, trusting Him to guide you.

Committing our actions and decisions to God grants wisdom and strength to walk in His purpose. Living out your purpose requires patience, faithfulness, and obedience to God's Word, even in uncertainty.

Staying faithful, obeying God's Word, and trusting Him leads to fulfilling His purpose.

CHAPTER ONE

DISCOVERING YOUR DIVINE PURPOSE

Understanding your divine purpose is essential for a focused life. Without direction, people often wander, feeling empty and frustrated. However, knowing your purpose brings clarity, joy, and fulfillment.

The biblical account of Moses illustrates this. Called to lead the Israelites out of Egypt, Moses initially doubted his abilities. Yet, God equipped him with strength and guidance, demonstrating that our purpose often involves serving others and fulfilling God's plans.

Each person is uniquely created with distinct gifts, talents, and experiences. Recognizing your individuality and the fact that you are *"wonderfully made"* [Psalm 139:14] helps you appreciate your purpose.

Discovering your purpose requires prayer and introspection. Spend time with God, asking Him to reveal His plans. The Holy Spirit is your guide, leading you to understand your purpose. Being attentive to His voice gives you clarity about what God desires for your life. This may come through a sense of peace, nudges in your heart, or confirmation from other believers.

Recognize that discovering your purpose is often a journey rather than an instant revelation. Life's experiences—both good and bad —shape your understanding of your purpose. Every experience contributes to fulfilling God's purpose in your life.

Discovering your divine purpose is vital. It brings clarity, direction, and a sense of belonging to God's grand design.

Seeking Clarity Through Prayer and Scripture

Uncertainty can cloud life's journey, making difficult decisions and traversing life's challenges. During these times, seeking clarity through prayer and Scripture is crucial. The Bible encourages us to turn to God in all situations.

Prayer is our direct line to God, allowing us to share fears, hopes, and questions. Constant communication keeps us connected to God and attuned to His guidance. When facing decisions, prayer seeks God's wisdom. As Proverbs 3:6 (NIV) advises, *"In all your ways submit to him, and he will make your paths straight."* Prayer opens our hearts to His direction, revealing the best choices.

In times of confusion, prayer brings peace. Laying concerns before God comforts us, as Isaiah 26:3 (NKJV) promises: *"You will keep him in perfect peace, whose mind is stayed on You because he trusts in You."* This peace enables clearer vision.

Prayer involves listening, not just talking. After presenting requests, silence allows God to speak. He may provide insight through thoughts, feelings, or impressions.

Scriptures illuminate our path, offering guidance and insight. Psalm 119:105 (ESV) says, *"Your word is a lamp to my feet and a light to my path."* Like Joseph, biblical accounts of individuals seeking God's direction teach us valuable lessons.

Engaging with Scripture through meditation aligns our minds with God's thoughts, clarifying His will. Praying through verses internalizes God's promises and truths. For example, praying 2 Timothy 1:7 (NLT), *"For God has not given us a spirit of fear and timidity, but of power and love and self-discipline,"* helps overcome fear.

Keeping a prayer journal tracks God's answers and clarity over time. Fasting can also enhance prayer life, increasing focus and removing distractions.

For instance, I recall a time when I faced a difficult decision. Through prayer and Scripture, I found clarity and peace. God's Word spoke directly to my situation, guiding me toward the right choice.

The Bible is filled with examples of individuals who sought clarity through prayer and Scripture. Take David, who wrote in Psalm 119:130 (AMP), *"The unfolding of Your words gives light; it gives understanding to the simple."* His experience demonstrates the power of Scripture in revealing God's will.

Understanding Your Unique Role in God's Plan

We have a distinct purpose within God's grand design, just as every body part serves a unique function (1 Corinthians 12:4-6). Recognizing this uniqueness leads to a more fulfilling and focused life.

The Bible emphasizes our individuality: *"We are fearfully and wonderfully made"* [Psalm 139:14, NIV], and God has specific plans to prosper us, giving us hope and a future (Jeremiah 29:11, NIV). Everyone possesses unique gifts and talents (1 Peter 4:10, NIV).

To understand your role, take time to reflect on your strengths. Do you have a talent for teaching, encouragement, or leadership? Seeking feedback from trusted friends or mentors can provide valuable insight into your strengths. Ask them what they believe you excel at and how you have positively impacted their lives.

In Romans 12:6-8, Paul talks about the various spiritual gifts within the church, such as prophecy, service, teaching, encouragement, giving, leadership, and mercy. Understanding these gifts can help you identify where you fit in God's plan.

God often places passions in our hearts that align with our

purpose. What excites you? What causes ignite in your spirit? Your passions can be clues to your role in God's plan. Colossians 3:23 encourages us to work at everything we do with all our hearts as if we are working for the Lord.

Consider how your passions can serve others. Mark 10:45 reminds us that even the Son of Man did not come to be served but to serve. Your unique role may be found in how you can help others through your passions and interests.

Understanding your unique role often involves listening to God's calling. John 10:27 states, *"My sheep hear my voice, and I know them, and they follow me"* (NIV). Spend time in prayer and reflection, asking God to reveal His purpose for you.

God often uses situations in our lives to guide us toward our calling. Pay attention to opportunities that arise and how they align with your gifts and passions. Isaiah 6:8 shows us how God seeks willing servants, saying, *"Whom shall I send? Here I am! Send me"* (NIV).

Finding your unique role is often a journey, not a destination. Philippians 1:6 reassures us that God, who began a good work in you, will carry it on to completion. Embrace the process of discovering and growing into your role.

Many struggle with fear and doubt regarding their purpose. Remember that *God does not give us a spirit of fear but of power, love, and a sound mind* [2 Timothy 1:7, NIV]. Trust in His ability to equip you for your role.

It's easy to compare our gifts and roles with those of others. However, Galatians 6:4 encourages us to examine our actions and not compare ourselves with others. Embrace the uniqueness of your journey.

As you seek to understand your role, challenges may arise. In 1 Corinthians 15:58, Paul encourages us to stand firm, let nothing move us, and always give ourselves entirely to the work of the

Lord. Stay committed to your journey, knowing that your labor in the Lord is not in vain.

A Life of Hope and Purpose

Jeremiah 29:11 (NIV) declares, *"For I know the plans I have for you," says the Lord, plans to prosper you and not to harm you, plans to give you hope and a future."* This reminds us that God has a specific purpose for our lives, filled with hope and promise. Understanding this can transform how we view our journey, especially during challenging times.

This verse was spoken to the Israelites during exile in Babylon. They felt lost, hopeless, and disconnected from their homeland. Through the prophet Jeremiah, God reassured them that despite their circumstances, He had a plan for their future. This context shows that God's promises remain faithful even in the darkest moments.

Recognizing that God is sovereign over our lives helps us trust in His plans. He is aware of our struggles and joys and desires us to thrive. As Psalm 139:16 (NKJV) says, *"Your eyes saw my substance, being yet unformed. And in Your book, they all were written, the days fashioned for me, when there were none yet."* This reminds us that our lives are part of a greater narrative that God is weaving together.

God's promise in Jeremiah 29:11 speaks of prosperity, which means well-being, success, and fulfillment. This doesn't always translate to material wealth but encompasses spiritual, emotional, and relational prosperity. God desires us to flourish in every aspect of our lives.

God's plans are not meant to bring harm but to build us up. Sometimes, we may face trials that feel painful or confusing. However, Romans 8:28 (ESV) says, *"And we know that for those who love God, all things work together for good."* Even when we don't understand our circumstances, we can trust that God works behind the scenes for our ultimate good.

God's promises extend beyond our present difficulties. He assures us that there is a hopeful future ahead. In Psalm 42:11 (NLT), *"Why, my soul, are you downcast? Why so disturbed within me? Put your hope in God, for I will yet praise him, my Savior and my God."* This encourages us to remain hopeful, knowing that brighter days are coming.

To live out God's plans, we must actively seek His guidance. Ephesians 2:10 (NIV) says, *"For we are God's handiwork, created in Christ Jesus to do good works, which God prepared in advance for us to do."* Embracing this truth allows us to step confidently into our calling.

Life is not always easy, and there will be obstacles along the way. Yet, James 1:2-4 (AMP) encourages us to *consider it pure joy whenever we face trials, knowing that testing our faith produces perseverance.* Trusting in God's plans gives us the strength to overcome these challenges.

CHAPTER TWO

THE DANGERS OF DISTRACTION

From smartphones and social media to endless notifications and busy schedules, it's easy to lose focus on what truly matters. Distraction can lead us away from our goals, relationships, and, most importantly, our purpose in life. As followers of Christ, we are called to live intentionally, keeping our eyes fixed on Him. In Hebrews 12:1-2 (NIV), "Let us throw off everything that hinders and the sin that so easily entangles. And let us run with perseverance the race marked out for us, fixing our eyes on Jesus, the pioneer and perfecter of faith." This focus is crucial in avoiding the dangers that distraction brings.

Distraction often leads to a loss of our sense of purpose. When we become consumed by what's happening around us, we can forget why we're here in the first place. When distractions take over, we might lose sight of those plans, leading us to drift aimlessly. It's essential to regularly remind ourselves of our God-given purpose and to stay committed to fulfilling it.

Distraction can significantly decrease our productivity. Studies have shown that it takes time to regain focus after being interrupted. When we allow distractions to take control, we waste precious time that could be spent on meaningful tasks. Being productive and focused in our daily tasks honors God and will enable us to progress toward our goals.

Distractions can strain our relationships with family, friends, and God. When we're not fully present, we miss valuable moments with loved ones. How often have we been at a dinner table, but everyone is glued to their phones instead of engaging with one another? We must invest time and attention into our relationships to grow together and support each other in faith.

Perhaps the most significant danger of distraction is spiritual drift. We may unintentionally neglect our relationship with God when we become too focused on the world's noise. If we allow distractions to take precedence, we can quickly lose the intimacy of our connection with God, leading to a shallow faith.

Distractions can also contribute to feelings of anxiety and stress. With so many competing demands on our attention, we may feel overwhelmed. In Matthew 6:34 (NKJV), Jesus encourages us not to worry about tomorrow, stating, *"Therefore do not worry about tomorrow, for tomorrow will worry about itself. Each day has enough trouble of its own."* Distracted, we can lose sight of living in the present and trusting God with our future.

Finding ways to minimize distractions and focus on what we can control is crucial. When distracted, our ability to make sound decisions can be compromised. We may rush into choices without prayerfully considering our options. Staying focused on God allows us to seek His wisdom in our decision-making processes.

Recognizing the Traps That Derail Your Focus

We must recognize the traps that can derail our focus as we strive to keep our eyes on God and our goals. 1 Peter 5:8 (NIV) reminds us, *"Be sober-minded; be watchful. Your adversary, the devil, prowls around like a roaring lion, seeking someone to devour."* Understanding these traps will empower us to stay focused on our divine purpose.

The Trap of Busyness:

One of the most common traps is busyness. We often equate being busy with being productive, but busyness can lead to exhaustion and burnout. Ecclesiastes 3:1 (NKJV) cautions, *"To everything, there is a season, a time for every purpose under heaven."* We must prioritize our tasks wisely, ensuring alignment with our God-given purpose. Regularly evaluating our commitments helps us avoid losing sight of what truly matters.

The Trap of Comparison:

In a world driven by social media and constant exposure to others' lives, comparison can quickly become a trap. We may measure our worth against others' successes, leading to feelings of inadequacy and discouragement. Galatians 6:4 (ESV) advises, *"Each one should test his own work, and then his reason to boast will be in himself alone and not in his neighbor."* Remembering that God has a unique plan for us helps us stay focused on our path and purpose.

The Trap of Perfectionism:

Perfectionism can be a significant roadblock to focus. The desire to achieve perfection in our work or relationships can lead to anxiety and procrastination. Matthew 5:48 (NLT) encourages, *"But you are to be perfect, even as your Father in heaven is perfect."* However, this doesn't mean we should be flawless; instead, it speaks to the completeness and maturity we find in Him. Embracing progress over perfection allows us to stay focused on our journey without being paralyzed by fear of failure.

The Trap of Negativity

Negative thoughts can easily creep into our minds, leading us away from focus and purpose. Whether it's self-doubt, fear of the future, or discouragement from past mistakes, negativity can weigh us down. *"Finally, brothers, whatever is true, whatever is noble, whatever is right, whatever is pure, whatever is lovely, whatever is admirable—if anything is excellent or praiseworthy—think about such things"* (Philippians 4:8, NIV). We can overcome negativity and maintain a hopeful perspective by focusing on positive thoughts and God's promises.

The Trap of Procrastination

Procrastination is another common trap that can derail our focus. Delaying essential tasks can lead to increased stress and feeling overwhelmed. *"The sluggard craves and gets nothing, while the soul of the diligent is richly supplied"* (Proverbs 13:4, NKJV). Taking small, actionable steps toward our goals can help us overcome procrastination and stay focused on what we need to accomplish.

The Trap of Overcommitment

Saying yes to every request can lead to over-commitment, which dilutes our focus and energy. While it's essential to serve others, we must also recognize our limits. *"Let your 'yes' be 'yes' and your 'no' be 'no'"* (Matthew 5:37, ESV). Setting healthy boundaries enables us to prioritize our time and efforts on what God has called us to do, allowing us to maintain our focus.

The Trap of Fear and Doubt

Fear and doubt can be paralyzing, causing us to second-guess our decisions and abilities. These emotions can distract us from our purpose and hinder our progress. *"For God gave us a spirit not of fear but of power and love and self-control"* (2 Timothy 1:7, NIV). By placing our trust in God's strength, we can confront our fears and move forward with confidence in our purpose.

How Satan Uses Distraction to Abort Destiny

Distraction is a powerful tool that the enemy, Satan, uses to divert our attention from God's purpose for our lives. By sowing seeds of confusion and chaos, he seeks to abort our destiny and prevent us from fulfilling the plans that God has set for us. *"The thief comes only to steal and kill and destroy; I have come that they may have life, and have it to the full"* (John 10:10, NIV).

One of the most significant distractions is the pursuit of worldly desires. *"Do not love the world or anything in the world. If anyone loves the world, love for the Father is not in them"* (1 John 2:15, NIV). We can lose sight of our divine purpose when consumed by materialism, status, or fleeting pleasures. Satan lures us into chasing these temporary gains, hoping to drown out the voice of God in our lives.

Fear and anxiety are potent distractions that can paralyze us and prevent us from stepping into our destiny. *"Do not be anxious about anything, but in every situation, by prayer and petition, with thanksgiving, present your requests to God"* (Philippians 4:6-7, NIV). When we allow fear to take root, it can cloud our judgment and lead us to make decisions that stray from God's path.

Negative influences from friends, media, or our environment can also derail our focus. *"Whoever walks with the wise becomes wise, but the companion of fools will suffer harm"* (Proverbs 13:20, NKJV). When we surround ourselves with negativity, it can seep into our minds and hearts, affecting our attitudes and decisions.

Holding onto unforgiveness and bitterness can be a significant distraction. *"See to it that no one fails to obtain the grace of God; that no 'root of bitterness' springs up and causes trouble"* (Hebrews 12:15, ESV). Unforgiveness can consume our thoughts and energy, leading us away from God's peace and purpose.

Comparison is another trap that can lead us away from our purpose. We can become discouraged or envious when we measure our worth against someone else's achievements. Satan uses comparison to distract us from appreciating our unique calling and gifts.

Doubt is a significant tool that Satan uses to derail our destiny. When we question God's promises or our abilities, we open the door to distraction. *"But when you ask, you must believe and not doubt, because the one who doubts is like a wave of the sea, blown and tossed by the wind"* (James 1:6, NIV). Doubt can lead us to second-guess our calling, hindering our ability to act on God's guidance.

Overcoming Spiritual Blockages

Spiritual blockages are barriers that hinder our relationship with God and obstruct our spiritual growth. These blockages can manifest as feelings of disconnect, doubt, or an inability to hear God's voice. Various factors, including sin, unresolved issues, or external influences, can cause them. *"But your iniquities have separated you from your God; your sins have hidden his face from you so that he will not hear"* (Isaiah 59:2, NIV). Thankfully, we can overcome these spiritual blockages through prayer, repentance, and intentional steps toward healing and restoration.

Before overcoming spiritual blockages, identifying their source is essential. *"Search me, God, and know my heart; test me and know my anxious thoughts. See if there is any offensive way in me and lead me in the way everlasting"* (Psalm 139:23-24, NIV). Take time for self-reflection and honesty before God. Acknowledge any unresolved conflicts, habits, or attitudes that might be causing distance in your spiritual walk.

Repentance is vital in overcoming spiritual blockages. *"If we confess our sins, he is faithful and just and will forgive us and purify us from all unrighteousness"* (1 John 1:9, NIV). Repentance involves a genuine turning away from sin and returning to God. When we humble ourselves and seek forgiveness, we open the door for God to restore our relationship with Him.

Prayer is a powerful tool for overcoming spiritual blockages. Through prayer, we invite God into our struggles and ask for His guidance, wisdom, and strength. Developing a consistent prayer life keeps us connected to God and enables Him to work in our hearts and minds.

God's Word is a source of strength and encouragement. *"For the word of God is alive and active, sharper than any two-edged sword"* (Hebrews 4:12, NIV). Immersing ourselves in Scripture provides insights and revelations to address our issues, bringing healing, clarity, and renewed purpose.

We are not meant to walk our spiritual journey alone. *"And let us consider how we may spur one another on toward love and good deeds, not giving up meeting together"* (Hebrews 10:24-25, NIV). Seeking support from fellow believers provides encouragement, accountability, and prayer.

Unresolved hurts from the past can create significant spiritual blockages. *"Get rid of all bitterness, rage and anger, brawling and slander, along with every form of malice. Be kind and compassionate to one another, forgiving each other, just as in Christ God forgave you"* (Ephesians 4:31-32, NIV). Letting go of grudges and past pain allows us to experience God's love and grace.

Worship is a powerful way to break through spiritual blockages. *"Enter his gates with thanksgiving and his courts with praise; give thanks to him and praise his name"* (Psalm 100:4, NIV). Worship shifts our focus from problems to God's greatness, inviting His presence and creating an environment for healing.

CHAPTER THREE

BUILDING A DISCIPLINED LIFE

Discipline is the foundation upon which a focused and purposeful life is built. It is not merely about strict routines or rigid schedules; instead, it is about developing habits that align with our values, goals, and God's purpose for our lives. "Do you not know that in a race all the runners run, but only one gets the prize? Run in such a way as to get the prize" (1 Corinthians 9:24-27, NIV). Building a life of discipline is essential for overcoming distractions and achieving the goals that God has set for us.

Discipline is making intentional choices that lead us closer to our goals and purpose. *"Whoever loves discipline loves knowledge"* (Proverbs 12:1, NIV). Embracing discipline allows us to grow in wisdom and understanding, helping us to make better decisions. It helps us prioritize what truly matters and avoid the pitfalls of procrastination and distractions.

To build a disciplined life, we must set clear, achievable goals. Specific goals give us direction and motivate us to stay focused. We should seek God's guidance when setting our goals, ensuring they align with His will for our lives. Reviewing these goals can help us stay accountable and adjust our paths as necessary.

Routines provide structure and stability, making it easier to cultivate discipline. *"The plans of the diligent lead surely to abundance"* (Proverbs 21:5, NKJV). Establishing daily and weekly routines can help us allocate time for prayer, study, work, and rest. Consistency in our routines fosters habits that support our goals.

Having accountability can significantly enhance our ability to stay disciplined. *"As iron sharpens iron, so one person sharpens another"* (Proverbs 27:17, NIV). Finding a mentor, friend, or accountability partner who shares similar goals can provide encouragement and support.

Discipline requires confronting and overcoming temptations that may lead us astray. Identifying the distractions or temptations in our lives allows us to develop strategies to resist them. A growth mindset is crucial for building a disciplined life. Embracing challenges and viewing failures as opportunities for growth will enable us to remain disciplined even when faced with setbacks.

While discipline is crucial, it is equally important to recognize the need for rest and balance. Building a disciplined life does not mean pushing ourselves to burnout. Incorporating rest into our routines ensures we recharge physically, mentally, and spiritually. Balance allows us to maintain our focus without losing sight of life's joy and fulfillment.

The Power of Consistency and Spiritual Growth

Just as a plant needs regular watering and sunlight to thrive, our relationship with God flourishes through consistent practices. *"Always give yourselves fully to the work of the Lord, because you know that your labor in the Lord is not in vain"* (1 Corinthians 15:58, NIV). This passage reminds us that consistency in our faith leads to growth and fruitfulness in our lives.

Daily spiritual practices, such as prayer, reading Scripture, and worship, are essential for nurturing our faith. *"But seek first his kingdom and his righteousness"* (Matthew 6:33, NIV). We create a strong foundation for spiritual growth by prioritizing our relationship with God daily.

To grow spiritually, we must cultivate healthy habits. Just as we develop routines for physical health, we must also establish routines for spiritual well-being. Setting clear spiritual goals can help us remain focused and motivated in our growth. *"I press on toward the goal to win the prize for which God has called me heavenward in Christ Jesus"* (Philippians 3:14, NIV).

Life often presents challenges that can disrupt our spiritual consistency. *"Consider it pure joy, my brothers and sisters, whenever you face trials of many kinds"* (James 1:2-4, NIV). Recognizing that challenges are a part of our growth journey helps us remain steadfast, even when circumstances are difficult.

Prayer is a cornerstone of spiritual growth. Consistent prayer deepens our relationship with God and helps us grow in trust and faith. Consistent engagement with God's Word is crucial for spiritual growth. The Scripture helps us gain wisdom and direction, enabling us to navigate life's challenges with faith.

As we commit to consistency in our spiritual practices, we begin to see the fruit of our labor. Consistency is directly linked to spiritual maturity. As we remain consistent in our faith practices, we become more mature in our understanding and relationship with God, allowing us to reflect His love to others more effectively.

Gaining Spiritual Wings

In Revelation 12:14, we read, *"But the woman was given the two wings of a great eagle, that she might fly into the wilderness, to her place, where she is nourished for a time and times and half a time, from the presence of the serpent"* (NKJV). This imagery represents divine protection and escapes amid adversity. Revelation 12 describes a cosmic battle between good and evil, where the woman represents God's people, and the dragon symbolizes Satan.

The wings of a great eagle signify strength and protection. Eagles are known for their ability to fly high and navigate harsh conditions. As Isaiah 40:31 reminds us, *"But those who wait on the Lord shall renew their strength; they shall mount up with wings like eagles*" (NKJV). When we rely on God, we gain strength to rise above our circumstances. Gaining spiritual wings means trusting God's power to uplift us during difficult times.

The wilderness is often seen as a place of testing and preparation. In this context, the woman is nourished in the wilderness, highlighting that God provides for us even in the most challenging environments. Just as the Israelites wandered in the wilderness and received manna from heaven (Exodus 16:4), we can trust that God will sustain us in our wilderness experiences. This nourishment comes through prayer, Scripture, and community, allowing us to grow spiritually.

The verse mentions that the woman flies to her "place," which signifies that God has a unique purpose and destination for each of us. Gaining spiritual wings means recognizing our place in God's plan and being willing to embrace it, even when it leads us through trials.

Faith is essential for gaining spiritual wings. We can rise above our doubts and fears when we trust God, even in uncertainty. Like the woman in Revelation, we must believe God will provide us with the strength and guidance to navigate our journey. The promise of nourishment in Revelation 12:14 signifies God's provision in times of need.

Just as the woman is nourished, God nourishes us spiritually through His Word, prayer, and the Holy Spirit. Gaining spiritual wings means relying on God for our sustenance, knowing He will fill us with what we need to thrive. The serpent represents the forces of evil that seek to hinder our spiritual growth. However, we can gain victory over these influences by staying close to God.

Gaining spiritual wings often requires embracing change. Just as eagles go through a molting process to grow new feathers, we must be willing to let go of old habits and mindsets that hold us back. *"And be transformed by the renewing of your mind"* (Romans 12:2, NKJV). This transformation allows us to soar higher in our faith and live out God's purpose.

Gaining spiritual wings brings us the joy of living according to God's will. When we trust Him and embrace our unique purpose, we experience the freedom to live a focused life. *"He satisfies your desires with good things so that your youth is renewed like the eagle's"* (Psalm 103:5, NKJV). Soaring in faith allows us to live with purpose, hope, and joy.

CHAPTER FOUR

RISING ABOVE PAIN AND BITTERNESS THROUGH INTERCESSION

I ntercession is the act of praying on behalf of someone else. It is a selfless act of love that mirrors the heart of Christ, who "is at the right hand of God and is also interceding for us" (Romans 8:34, NIV). We step into their lives and needs when we pray for others, bridging their struggles and God's promises.

When we intercede for others, we move the focus away from our worries and challenges. *"Each of you should look not only to your interests but also to the interests of others"* (Philippians 2:4, NIV). By doing this, we cultivate a heart of compassion and selflessness. As we pray for the needs of friends, family, or even strangers, our concerns diminish, and we are reminded that we are part of a larger community.

Intercessory prayer nurtures empathy and compassion within us. *"Rejoice with those who rejoice; mourn with those who mourn"* (Romans 12:15, NIV). When we take the time to understand the struggles of others, we develop a deeper connection to their experiences. As we pray for their needs, we become more aware of their challenges, strengthening our ability to love and support them.

Intercessory prayer is a powerful way to communicate with God. *"The prayer of a righteous person is powerful and effective"* (James 5:16, NIV). As we pray for others, we profoundly experience God's faithfulness and love, which helps restore our focus on His goodness and grace.

Praying for others often leads to personal clarity and direction. As we seek God's guidance for their lives, we may find answers to our questions. *"Trust in the Lord with all your heart and lean not on your understanding"* (Proverbs 3:5-6, NIV). When we intercede, we surrender our desires and allow God to lead us.

Interceding for others fosters a sense of unity within our communities. *"Consider how we may spur one another on toward love and good deeds"* (Hebrews 10:24-25, NIV). When we pray together, we create a supportive environment where love and encouragement flourish.

We witness God's work in their lives as we pray for others. *"Rejoice always, pray continually, give thanks in all circumstances"* (1 Thessalonians 5:16-18, NIV). Witnessing God's faithfulness in the lives of others restores our focus on His power and love.

Interceding for others often leads to personal growth. As we pray, we may feel prompted to take action, offer support, or reach out to those in need. *"Speak the truth in love, growing in every way into him who is the head"* (Ephesians 4:15, NIV). This growth benefits those we pray for and helps us develop into the people God created us to be.

Intercessory prayer can heal and restore our hearts. When we pray for others, we may find our burdens lightened and our spirits uplifted. As we intercede, we release our worries and allow God to comfort us.

When we intercede for others, we empower them to seek God for themselves. Our prayers can inspire them to deepen their faith and reliance on God. As we lift others in prayer, we invite them into a relationship with God, helping them discover His purpose for their lives.

Interceding for others is a call to be prayer warriors in our communities. God desires for us to stand in the gap for those in need. As we answer this call, we become vessels of God's grace and love, restoring focus not only in our own lives but also in the lives of others.

Overcoming Family Challenges and Emotional Pain

Family is often considered a source of love and support, but it can also be a source of challenges and emotional pain. Each family faces unique difficulties due to conflict, misunderstanding, loss, or other struggles. The first step in overcoming family challenges is acknowledging that they exist. It's essential to recognize that no family is perfect and that conflicts can arise in many forms, including disagreements over values, lifestyle choices, and misunderstandings.

"I praise you because I am fearfully and wonderfully made" (Psalm 139:14, NIV). This reminder helps us accept our differences as part of God's design and approach challenges with compassion rather than judgment.

Turning to God for guidance in times of family challenges is essential. Through prayer, we can seek God's perspective on our situations, asking for His guidance on responding to conflicts and emotional pain. Effective communication is crucial in overcoming family challenges. When communicating with family members, listening actively and expressing our feelings honestly is essential without resorting to hurtful words or accusations.

Practicing open and respectful dialogue can foster understanding and create a safe space for healing. Forgiveness is vital in healing within families. Holding onto grudges and past hurts only prolongs emotional pain and conflict. When we choose to forgive, we release resentment and open the door for healing.

Establishing healthy boundaries is essential in maintaining emotional well-being within families. Boundaries help protect our emotional health and prevent toxic behaviors from affecting our lives. Sometimes, family challenges can feel overwhelming, and seeking professional help can provide valuable support.

Counselors and therapists can offer guidance in navigating emotional pain and resolving conflicts. As we work through family challenges, it's essential to embrace the process of healing. Healing takes time and requires patience, understanding, and a willingness to change.

Allowing God to work in our hearts can lead to renewed relationships and emotional wholeness. Overcoming challenges can ultimately strengthen family bonds. *"Be devoted to one another in love. Honor one another above yourselves"* (Romans 12:10, NIV).

When we commit to working through challenges, we can build a foundation of love and support that enriches our family relationships. Holding onto God's promises is essential amid family challenges and emotional pain. Focusing on His promises gives us hope that transcends our circumstances.

This hope gives us the strength to face challenges and believe in the possibility of healing. Faith plays a crucial role in overcoming family challenges. Trusting in God's ability to heal our families can empower us to take the necessary steps toward restoration.

When we believe in God, we open our hearts to the transformative work of the Holy Spirit.

Joseph's Journey: From Rejection to Restoration

Joseph's journey begins with rejection from his own family. As the favored son of Jacob, he received a beautiful coat of many colors, stirring jealousy and resentment among his brothers (Genesis 37:3-4).

This favoritism culminated in a betrayal when his brothers

plotted against him, selling him into slavery and deceiving their father into believing Joseph was dead (Genesis 37:18-30). This act of rejection was not just a physical separation but a deep emotional wound.

In Egypt, Joseph faced further trials as an enslaved person in Potiphar's house. Despite his circumstances, Joseph worked diligently and gained Potiphar's trust, becoming the overseer of his household (Genesis 39:4).

However, temptation struck when Potiphar's wife falsely accused him of wrongdoing, leading to imprisonment (Genesis 39:7-20). This was another layer of rejection, yet Joseph's integrity and reliance on God shone through.

While in prison, Joseph interpreted the dreams of Pharaoh's cupbearer and baker, revealing his God-given gift (Genesis 40:14-19). Despite circumstances, Joseph remained faithful and used his talents to serve others.

His ability to interpret dreams eventually led him to Pharaoh, accurately predicting seven years of plenty followed by seven years of famine (Genesis 41:14-30). This moment marked a significant turning point in Joseph's journey.

Joseph's interpretation led to his elevation to second-in-command in Egypt (Genesis 41:46). This transformation illustrates how God can turn rejection and trials into opportunities for restoration and influence.

Joseph's rise to power positioned him to save his family and many others from famine. God had a divine plan for Joseph, demonstrating that struggles can prepare us for future blessings.

Years later, during the famine, Joseph's brothers came to Egypt seeking food. This reunion was filled with tension, as they did not recognize him. Joseph had the opportunity to seek revenge but chose the path of forgiveness (Genesis 45:4-15).

He revealed his identity and said God had sent him to preserve their lives. This act of forgiveness showcased Joseph's growth and understanding of God's plan, transforming rejection into reconciliation. Joseph's story does not end with forgiveness; it extends to restoration. He invited his family to live in Egypt, providing for them during the famine (Genesis 47:11-12). This act of love and provision brought healing to their broken family.

Joseph's journey teaches us that restoration often involves bringing those who have wronged us back into our lives with love and grace. The journey from rejection to restoration emphasizes trusting God's plan, even when the path is difficult. Even in the face of betrayal and hardship, his unwavering faith encourages us to trust that God is working behind the scenes.

CHAPTER FIVE

OVERCOMING BITTERNESS TO FULFILL DESTINY

Bitterness can be a heavy weight on the soul, hindering spiritual growth and delaying the fulfillment of God's purpose in our lives. It often arises from deep pain, betrayal, or disappointment, and if left unchecked, it can consume us, keeping us from experiencing the fullness of God's plan.

It often takes root when we feel wronged or hurt by others. These feelings can linger when we hold onto resentment, focusing on what has been done to us instead of how we can move forward. If not addressed, bitterness can grow into something that contaminates every part of our lives, affecting our relationships, mindset, and even our health.

Holding onto bitterness distorts our perspective and limits our ability to move forward. Instead of looking ahead, we become trapped in the past, replaying the hurtful experiences repeatedly. This prevents us from growing spiritually and can block God's blessings.

Bitterness also clouds our decision-making, making it difficult to follow God's lead or hear His voice. We may even miss divine opportunities because we are too focused on the pain of the past.

In Ephesians 4:31-32, Paul urges believers to *"get rid of all bitterness, rage and anger, brawling and slander, along with every form of malice. Be kind and compassionate to one another, forgiving each other, just as in Christ God forgave you"* (NIV). Only when we release bitterness can we experience the peace and freedom necessary to walk into our destiny.

After being betrayed by his brothers, sold into slavery, falsely accused, and imprisoned, Joseph had every reason to be bitter. Yet, Joseph trusted God through his trials and maintained a forgiving heart. When the opportunity arose for revenge, Joseph instead forgave his brothers and acknowledged God's hand in his journey.

He told them, *"You intended to harm me, but God intended it for good to accomplish what is now being done, the saving of many lives"* (Genesis 50:20, NIV). Joseph's refusal to let bitterness take root allowed him to fulfill his destiny. He rose to great authority in Egypt and saved his family and an entire nation from famine.

His story shows that even when others intend to harm us, God can use those circumstances if we remain focused on Him, not our pain. Forgiveness is the key to overcoming bitterness.

When we forgive those who wronged us, we release bitterness's hold on our lives. This doesn't mean the pain disappears immediately, but it begins the healing process.

Jesus teaches us, *"For if you forgive other people when they sin against you, your heavenly Father will also forgive you"* (Matthew 6:14-15, NIV). Holding onto bitterness harms us and hinders our relationship with God.

Forgiveness frees us from the chains of the past and opens the door for us to walk into our destiny. When we let go of the desire for revenge and trust God to deal with the injustices we've faced, we create space for His grace and blessings to flow into our lives.

Just as Christ forgave us, we are called to forgive others, not for their sake, but for our freedom and spiritual growth.

Letting go of bitterness requires surrendering it to God. This means acknowledging the pain and the hurt but trusting that God is in control and will bring justice in His perfect time.

"Do not take revenge, my dear friends, but leave room for God's wrath, for it is written: 'It is mine to avenge; I will repay,' says the Lord" (Romans 12:19, NIV). When we surrender our bitterness to God, we allow Him to work in our hearts and heal us from the inside out.

When we overcome bitterness, we allow God to pour His blessings and guide us toward our destiny. A life free of bitterness is marked by peace, joy, and spiritual growth.

It allows us to live fully in the present without the burden of past hurts weighing us down. As we walk in forgiveness and release bitterness, we can experience the abundant life that Jesus promises: *"The thief comes only to steal and kill and destroy; I have come that they may have life, and have it to the full"* (John 10:10, NIV).

Moreover, overcoming bitterness positions us to be used by God in powerful ways. When our pain no longer consumes us, we can focus on the calling God has placed on our lives.

We become more effective in our ministries, relationships, and personal growth. Our testimonies of overcoming bitterness can inspire others to do the same, leading to a ripple effect of healing and restoration.

How Bitterness Can Hinder Your Purpose

Bitterness starts small—maybe through an offense, hurt, or betrayal. But if we allow it to fester, it grows like a poison, slowly affecting every area of our lives. *"See to it that no one falls short of the grace of God and that no bitter root grows up to cause trouble and defile many"* (Hebrews 12:15, NIV). This warning emphasizes the danger of allowing bitterness to take root.

Like a plant that grows underground, bitterness spreads into other areas of our hearts, feeding on anger, resentment, and unforgiveness. Once bitterness takes root, it distorts our perspective. It clouds our ability to see God's goodness and traps us in the past, continually replaying the pain we've experienced.

Over time, bitterness causes us to focus more on the hurt than on healing, more on the wrong done to us than on the future God has for us. When bitterness takes over, it can block us from seeing and following God's will for our lives. Instead of being open to His direction, we become stuck in negative emotions, affecting our decisions and relationships.

When we refuse to forgive, we stay locked in the past, holding on to the hurt. This can cause us to miss the opportunities and blessings that God wants to give us.

After being freed from Egypt, the Israelites allowed bitterness and grumbling to creep in, even though God had promised them a land of blessing. Their bitterness closed their eyes to God's provision and delayed their journey to the Promised Land.

Like the Israelites, when we allow bitterness to control us, we can delay the fulfillment of God's promises in our lives. Bitterness affects our relationship with God and damages our relationships with others.

When we are bitter, we may begin to view people through a lens of suspicion, mistrust, and resentment. This can cause division and destroy the unity God calls us to have with others.

If we don't let go of bitterness, it can create a barrier between us and others, making it difficult to show love, compassion, and grace. Healthy relationships are necessary for fulfilling our God-given purpose.

If bitterness poisons our relationships, we may lose the support, encouragement, and fellowship we need to move forward in God's plan.

Bitterness also hinders spiritual growth. It prevents us from experiencing the peace and joy of a close relationship with God.

Bitterness blocks our communication with God and makes it difficult to hear His voice. Clinging to resentment shows a lack of faith in God's ability to bring justice or healing.

Instead of releasing the pain to Him, we take matters into our own hands, which stunts our spiritual growth.

To overcome bitterness and walk in the fullness of God's purpose, we must first recognize that we need God's help.

It is often difficult to forgive and let go of deep hurts, but with God's grace, it is possible.

Jesus provided the perfect example of forgiveness when He prayed for those who crucified Him, saying, *"Father, forgive them, for they know not what they do"* (Luke 23:34, NIV).

His willingness to forgive even in extreme suffering is a powerful reminder that we are called to forgive others, regardless of offense.

Prayer is vital to overcoming bitterness. We can ask God to soften our hearts, help us forgive, and release the hurt when bitterness tries to creep in.

When we bring our bitterness to God, He exchanges it for His peace.

Reflecting on God's Word can help heal our hearts. Scripture reminds us of God's promises, justice, and ability to bring good out of painful situations (*"And we know that in all things God works for the good of those who love him,"* Romans 8:28, NIV).

Choosing Forgiveness and Healing

Jesus emphasizes the importance of forgiveness throughout the New Testament. In *"For if you forgive others their trespasses, your heavenly Father will also forgive you, but if you do not forgive others their trespasses, neither will your Father forgive your trespasses"* (Matthew 6:14-15, NIV), He says. Forgiveness is not optional for a believer.

Forgiveness is central to our relationship with God because He has forgiven us first through Christ. Choosing to forgive is an act of obedience and faith. It involves trusting God to bring justice and healing in His perfect way and timing.

When we release others from their wrongs, we also trust God to take care of the hurt, knowing He will restore and vindicate us according to His will. Forgiveness sets us free from the emotional and spiritual burdens of holding onto hurt and bitterness.

When we refuse to forgive, we are the ones who suffer. We may feel anger, resentment, and even depression, all of which can affect our spiritual health and well-being.

However, forgiveness brings release. It takes away the weight of the pain, allowing us to experience God's peace and joy again. When we choose to forgive, we rid ourselves of the negative emotions from unresolved conflict and make room for kindness and compassion to grow in our hearts.

True healing can only occur when we let go of the offense and allow God to work in our hearts. Holding onto unforgiveness can often create spiritual blockages that keep us from experiencing the fullness of God's love and grace.

When we forgive, it clears the way for God to heal our wounds and restore what was lost. Our God is our ultimate healer, but we must be willing to release the hurt for Him to do His work in us.

When we forgive, we invite God's healing power into our lives, allowing Him to mend our hearts and restore our peace. Forgiveness also helps us to see situations through God's eyes.

It enables us to move beyond our pain and recognize how God can bring good out of every difficult circumstance. When we choose to forgive, we reflect God's character.

God is a forgiving God who calls us to extend that same grace to others. Jesus demonstrated the ultimate act of forgiveness on the cross when He said, *"Father, forgive them, for they do not know what they are doing"* (Luke 23:34, NIV).

Despite the pain and suffering He endured, He chose to forgive those who were responsible for His death. As followers of Christ, we are called to follow His example.

"Bear with each other and forgive one another if any of you has a grievance against someone. Forgive as the Lord forgave you" (Colossians 3:13, NIV). This kind of forgiveness is not always easy, especially when the hurt runs deep, but it is a powerful testimony of God's grace at work in us.

When we forgive, we show the world what it means to live like Christ. Forgiving not only heals our hearts but also has the power to restore broken relationships.

Many relationships suffer because of unresolved conflicts and unforgiveness. However, when one person takes the step to forgive, it can pave the way for reconciliation and healing.

This is especially important in families and marriages, where wounds often run deep. In Matthew 18:21-22, Peter asked Jesus how usually he should forgive someone who wrongs him.

Jesus replied, *"I tell you, not seven times, but seventy-seven times."* This response shows that forgiveness should be a continual process, especially in close relationships.

By choosing to forgive repeatedly, we allow God to bring healing and restoration to our relationships, which reflects His love and grace.

CHAPTER SIX

ALIGNING WITH GOD'S PROPHETIC PLAN

God's prophetic instruction is His direct guidance, given through His Word, dreams, visions, or the voice of the Holy Spirit. In the Bible, we see examples of God speaking through prophets like Isaiah, Jeremiah, and Elijah, offering specific directions and promises to His people.

These instructions were often critical to the success and survival of those who followed them. For example, in Genesis 41, Joseph interpreted Pharaoh's dreams as a warning of a coming famine. Joseph's ability to understand and follow this instruction not only saved Egypt but also preserved his family and brought him into a position of leadership.

For us today, prophetic instruction can come through Scripture, prayer, godly counsel, or the conviction of the Holy Spirit. When we are in tune with God, we will recognize His voice and understand His direction for our lives.

One key principle in aligning with God's prophetic instruction is obedience. When God gives us a prophetic word or a direction for our lives, we must act on it with faith and obedience.

A powerful example of this is found in the story of Noah. *"Then God said to Noah, 'I have decided to put an end to all flesh, for the earth is filled with violence because of them; now I will destroy them along with the earth. Make yourself an ark of gopher wood"* (Genesis 6:13-14, NIV); God gave Noah specific instructions.

Despite others' ridicule and doubt, Noah followed God's command. His obedience to the prophetic instruction saved his family and preserved humanity.

God may give us specific instructions in our lives, whether through a Scripture verse, a word from a pastor, or a personal conviction. Our responsibility is to respond obediently, trusting that God's plan is for our good.

Aligning with God's prophetic instruction also requires patience and trust in His timing. Sometimes, God reveals a prophetic word or promise, but the fulfillment of that word takes time.

In these seasons of waiting, we must remain faithful and focus on God's plan, even when we don't see immediate results.

Abraham is a powerful example of someone who had to wait on God's prophetic promise. In *"The Lord had said to Abram, 'Leave your country, your people and your father's household and go to the land I will show you'"* (Genesis 12:1, NIV), God promised Abraham that He would make him the father of many nations.

However, it took years before Abraham and Sarah had their son, Isaac. During this time, Abraham had to trust God's timing and remain faithful, even when the promise seemed delayed.

When we are waiting for the fulfillment of God's prophetic word in our lives, we must remember that His timing is perfect. *"But those who hope in the Lord will renew their strength. They will soar on wings like eagles; they will run and not grow weary; they will walk and not be faint"* (Isaiah 40:31, NIV).

Waiting is not passive but an active trust in God's perfect plan.

Aligning with God's prophetic instruction often involves stepping out in faith, even when the path ahead is unclear.

Doubt and fear can become obstacles to following God's direction. We may question whether we heard from God or worry about the risks of stepping out in faith.

Joshua, who led the Israelites into the Promised Land, is an excellent example of overcoming fear and doubt.

God encourages Joshua, *"Have I not commanded you? Be strong and courageous. Do not be afraid; do not be discouraged, for the Lord your God will be with you wherever you go"* (Joshua 1:9, NIV).

Despite the challenges ahead, Joshua aligned himself with God's prophetic instruction and led his people to victory.

When we align ourselves with God's prophetic instruction, we position ourselves to receive His blessings and fulfill our purpose.

"The Lord makes firm the steps of the one who delights in him" (Psalm 37:23, NIV). God delights in leading us; when we follow His lead, we experience His favor and success.

Joseph's life is a testimony of this truth. Despite his trials and setbacks, Joseph remained aligned with God's prophetic plan.

In the end, Joseph was elevated to great authority in Egypt, and God's promises to him were fulfilled.

When we follow God's prophetic instruction, even through difficult circumstances, His promises will come to pass in our lives.

It may not always happen in the way we expect, but God's plan is always for our good and His glory.

How to Discern and Respond to God's Guidance

God desires to lead us, just as a shepherd leads his sheep (*"My sheep listen to my voice; I know them, and they follow me,"* John 10:27, NIV), and He provides direction through His Word, prayer, the Holy Spirit, and sometimes through other people or circumstances.

One of the most reliable ways to discern God's guidance is by regularly engaging with Scripture. The Bible is God's Word and serves as a direct source of wisdom and instruction for our lives. *"Your word is a lamp for my feet, a light on my path"* (Psalm 119:105, NIV).

When we immerse ourselves in God's Word, we align our hearts with His desires and better recognize His direction. Scripture is filled with principles that guide our decisions, whether choosing between right and wrong or seeking wisdom for life's complex challenges.

If we are unsure about a situation, turning to the Bible can clarify and reinforce the choices we need to make. For example, when faced with decisions about relationships, work, or personal conduct.

Prayer is another powerful way to discern God's guidance. *"Do not be anxious about anything, but in every situation, by prayer and petition, with thanksgiving, present your requests to God"* (Philippians 4:6, NIV).

In prayer, we communicate with God, seeking His will and asking for clarity in our decisions. Prayer is not just about asking for things; it's about developing a relationship with God and learning to listen to Him.

When we quiet our hearts before God, He speaks to us through a sense of peace, a firm conviction, or by bringing certain Scriptures to mind. It's essential to create space in our prayer life to listen, not just to speak.

For instance, *"While they were worshiping the Lord and fasting, the Holy Spirit said, 'Set apart for me Barnabas and Saul for the work to which I have called them'"* (Acts 13:2-3, NIV), the Holy Spirit gave clear guidance to the early church leaders.

Through prayer, we, too, can receive direction from God about His plans for us.

The Holy Spirit plays a crucial role in guiding believers. *"When the Spirit of truth comes, He will guide you into all the truth"* (John 16:13, NIV).

The Holy Spirit is our constant companion, providing discernment, wisdom, and understanding. Being sensitive to the Holy Spirit involves having an open heart to His leading.

Often, the Spirit will prompt us through a nudge in our conscience, an inner sense of peace, or even discomfort when we go in the wrong direction. Following these prompts helps us stay on the path God has for us.

A key to being led by the Holy Spirit is maintaining a life of surrender to God's will. When we seek our desires over His, it becomes harder to hear His voice.

But when we remain open to His leading, even when it requires sacrifice, we can follow Him confidently.

Another way God often provides guidance is through the wisdom of others. *"Where there is no guidance, a people falls, but in an abundance of counselors there is safety"* (Proverbs 11:14, NIV).

Seeking advice from godly friends, mentors, or leaders can help us discern God's will, especially when we face difficult or complex situations.

Sometimes, God will confirm His direction for us through the counsel of others who have walked closely with Him. Their experience and knowledge of God's Word can offer fresh perspectives and help us see things we may have overlooked.

It's essential, however, that the advice we receive aligns with Scripture and that those we seek counsel from are spiritually mature and grounded in their faith.

God also speaks to us through our circumstances. He may open or close doors to guide us toward the right path or allow certain events to occur to teach us lessons or steer us in a specific direction.

While we must be careful not to base all decisions solely on circumstances, paying attention to how things unfold can often provide insight into God's will.

In *"Paul and his companions traveled throughout the region of Phrygia and Galatia, having been kept by the Holy Spirit from preaching the word in the province of Asia"* (Acts 16:6-10, NIV), Paul and his companions understood God's direction.

In the same way, God can orchestrate circumstances in our lives to make His will clear. When we experience closed doors or delays, instead of becoming discouraged, we should trust that God is working behind the scenes. *"And we know that in all things God works for the good of those who love Him, who have been called according to His purpose"* (Romans 8:28, NIV).

Whether favorable or not, every circumstance is part of God's perfect plan for our lives. Once we discern God's guidance, the next step is to respond in faith and obedience. Sometimes, God's direction will challenge us to step out of our comfort zone or to trust Him for something that seems impossible. *"Without faith, it is impossible to please God"* (Hebrews 11:6, NIV), and this faith requires action.

When God called Abraham to leave his homeland, He didn't provide a detailed plan. Abraham responded in faith, trusting God to lead him every step of the way.

Similarly, when we sense God's leading, we may not have all the answers, but stepping out in obedience will unlock His provision and blessings.

Responding to God's guidance also means staying patient when the answer doesn't come immediately. God's timing is perfect; sometimes, He asks us to wait and trust Him while He works things out behind the scenes.

Examples from David's Life

Before David ever sat on the throne, he was a shepherd. His early life caring for sheep might have seemed unimportant compared to the grandeur of being a king, but during these years, David developed qualities that would later help him fulfill his divine assignment.

David learned how to lead, protect, and nurture the sheep under his care, which were necessary for leading the people of Israel. David also developed a close relationship with God in the quiet fields, which was crucial to his success.

He spent time in worship, writing psalms, and learning to trust God in solitude. *Jesus teaches, "Whoever is faithful with very little will also be faithful with much" (Luke 16:10, NIV).*

David's story shows that God often uses humble beginnings to prepare us for more significant assignments. Before we step into prominent roles, we must prove faithful in God's small tasks.

One of the most defining moments of David's life was his battle with Goliath. While the entire army of Israel trembled in fear before the giant, David, still a young shepherd, stepped forward in faith, confident in God's power.

His courage came from his deep trust in God, which he developed during his years in the fields. *"You come against me with sword and spear and javelin, but I come against you in the name of the Lord Almighty... for the battle is the Lord's"* (1 Samuel 17:45-47, NIV).

This moment of victory showed that David understood his assignment wasn't about his strength but about trusting God's power.

We all face "giants" in our lives—challenges that seem impossible to overcome. David's story reminds us that even the most significant obstacles can be overcome when we rely on God.

After David's victory over Goliath, he didn't immediately become king. It was many years before he would take the throne, and much of that time was spent in the wilderness, running from King

Saul.

This period of David's life was marked by hardship but also a time of preparation. During his time in the wilderness, David learned to depend on God in ways he hadn't before.

During this period, he wrote many psalms, expressing his heart to God, seeking refuge in Him, and learning to trust God's promises even when circumstances looked bleak.

"I cry out to God Most High, to God who fulfills his purpose for me" (Psalm 57:2, NIV), David wrote.

Even in difficult seasons, David believed that God was working out His divine purpose in his life.

The wilderness can feel like a place of delay, but it is often where God molds us, refines our character, and prepares us for what's ahead.

One of the greatest lessons from David's life is the importance of waiting on God's timing.

Though he was anointed as king while still a boy, it was many years before he took the throne. During that time, David had opportunities to take matters into his own hands.

Yet David refused to do so, understanding that fulfilling his divine assignment meant trusting God's timing, not forcing things to happen.

"The Lord forbid that I should do such a thing to my master, the Lord's anointed" (1 Samuel 24, NIV).

David respected God's process and chose to wait for God to elevate him at the right time.

Waiting can be one of the most complex parts of discovering and fulfilling our purpose.

"Be still before the Lord and wait patiently for Him" (Psalm 37:7, NIV).

David's life shows us that when we wait on God's timing, the result is far greater than anything we could achieve by rushing ahead.

When David finally became king, he ruled with a heart after God's own.

He wasn't perfect, and his life included moments of failure, but throughout his reign, David remained devoted to fulfilling God's purpose for Israel.

He sought to honor God in his leadership, establish justice, and bring the nation back to worshipping the Lord.

David's reign shows us that fulfilling our divine assignment is not about perfection but a heart of obedience and repentance.

Even in his failures, David returned to God, seeking forgiveness and restoration.

"Have mercy on me, O God, according to your unfailing love; according to your great compassion, blot out my transgressions" (Psalm 51:1, NIV).

Focused Faith – Walking into Your Destiny

Trusting God beyond what you can see requires a deep level of faith that is not dependent on circumstances or visible signs. This type of trust is built on the knowledge of God's character, His promises, and His faithfulness throughout history. It's a trust that says, "Even when I don't know the way, I believe God does." *"Trust in the Lord with all your heart and lean not on your understanding; in all your ways submit to Him, and He will make your paths straight"* (Proverbs 3:5-6, NIV). One of the most significant challenges we face as believers is learning to walk by faith, not sight, as 2 Corinthians 5:7 teaches. We tend to trust what we can see, feel, or comprehend. God often calls us to trust Him in situations that don't make sense to our natural minds.

God promised Abraham that he would be the father of many nations, even though Abraham was old and his wife Sarah was barren. For years, they saw no evidence of that promise coming to pass. Yet Abraham trusted God beyond what he could see. He believed that the God who made the promise was faithful to fulfill it, even when his circumstances seemed impossible (Romans 4:18-21, NIV)—trusting God beyond what you can see means believing in His promises even when the evidence hasn't yet appeared. It's holding on to His Word, knowing He will bring it to pass in His perfect timing.

Fear is one of the biggest obstacles to trusting God beyond what you can see. When we face uncertain situations, fear can creep in and cause us to doubt God's goodness or plan for our lives. But the Bible repeatedly encourages us to "fear not" because God is with us. When fear arises, we must turn to God and trust Him. Trust is the antidote to fear. As we focus on God's power, love, and faithfulness, we are reminded that He is greater than any fear or uncertainty we may face. Trusting God beyond what you can see means having faith in His ability to carry you through every challenge, even when fear tries to shake your confidence.

When the Israelites were trapped between the Red Sea and the Egyptian army, it seemed like there was no way out. But Moses trusted God's instruction to "stand firm" and watch His deliverance. God parted the sea and made a way where there was no way (Exodus 14:13-14, NIV).

Moses' trust in God led to a miraculous victory. Joseph's life was filled with setbacks—being sold into slavery by his brothers, wrongly imprisoned, and forgotten. Yet, through it all, Joseph trusted God's plan for his life.

Eventually, God elevated him to a position of power in Egypt. Joseph realized that everything he went through was part of God's bigger plan to save his family and many others (Genesis 50:20, NIV). God gave the Israelites an unusual battle plan for taking the city of Jericho—marching around the city walls for seven days and shouting on the last day. It didn't make sense from a human perspective, but they trusted God's instruction, so the walls came down (Joshua 6:1-5, NIV). Their obedience and trust led to victory.

One of the biggest challenges in trusting God beyond what we can see is letting go of control. As humans, we like to plan, organize, and predict outcomes. But when it comes to following God, He often asks us to surrender our control and trust His plans.

Trusting God means believing His plans are better than anything we could imagine, even when we can't see how things will work out. It's about releasing our grip on the situation and allowing God to guide us according to His will.

Surrendering control doesn't mean we stop making decisions or being responsible. Instead, it means we invite God into the process and trust that His wisdom and guidance will lead us in the right direction.

Trusting God beyond what you can see also applies during times of waiting. Waiting is often one of the most challenging aspects of faith because we don't know when or how God will act. Yet, waiting is a crucial part of the faith journey. *"But those who wait on the Lord shall renew their strength; they shall mount up with wings like eagles, they shall run and not be weary, they shall walk and not faint"* (Isaiah 40:31, NIV).

In the waiting, God is working. He is shaping our character, preparing us for the next step, and aligning circumstances for His perfect timing. Trusting God during seasons of waiting means believing that He is faithful and that His timing is always best, even when we grow impatient.

While faith gives us a sense of direction and purpose, focus keeps us moving toward that goal. Focus allows us to concentrate on what truly matters, filtering out distractions and competing priorities. As *"whatever is true, whatever is noble, whatever is right, whatever is pure, whatever is lovely, whatever is admirable —if anything is excellent or praiseworthy—think about such things"* (Philippians 4:8, NIV), we prioritize our thoughts and actions.

Maintaining focus makes us more likely to take meaningful steps toward our goals. It helps us prioritize our time and energy, ensuring we invest in activities aligning with our faith and purpose.

This focused mindset is crucial in a world filled with distractions, as it helps us avoid losing sight of God's plan for our lives. Faith and focus are interconnected. Focusing on His purpose for our lives becomes easier when we have faith in God's promises. Conversely, our faith is strengthened when we clearly focus on God's plans.

The story of Peter walking on water illustrates this concept (Matthew 14:22-33). When Peter focused on Jesus, he could step out of the boat and walk on the water.

However, he began to sink when he shifted his focus to the wind and waves. This demonstrates how our focus can directly impact our ability to live out our faith. We can accomplish incredible things by keeping our eyes on Jesus and His promises. But when distractions and doubts creep in, they can cause us to falter.

Therefore, nurturing our faith and focus is essential for a successful spiritual journey. Integrating faith and focus into our daily lives can have a transformative impact. We become more resilient in the face of challenges, more confident in our decisions, and more aligned with God's will. This alignment affects not only us personally but also those around us.

We become role models for our families, friends, and communities as we demonstrate faith and focus. Our unwavering trust in God inspires others to develop their faith and focus, creating a ripple effect of positive change.

Ascending to New Realms of Influence

"After this, I looked, and there before me was a door standing open in heaven. And the voice I had first heard speaking to me like a trumpet said, 'Come up here, and I will show you what must take place after

this." (Revelation 4:1, NIV).

The phrase *"Come up here"* signifies an invitation from God to rise above our current circumstances. It encourages us to seek a deeper relationship with Him, gaining insight and clarity. God often calls us to rise above our challenges, fears, and distractions.

To ascend means to elevate our thinking, actions, and understanding. It is about moving away from the mundane and entering into God's divine presence, where we can experience His wisdom and guidance.

When we ascend spiritually, we are elevated in our relationship with God and empowered to influence our surroundings positively. As we grow in faith, we become beacons of hope and light to others. Our lives reflect God's love and grace, encouraging those around us to seek Him. *"Let your light shine before others, that they may see your good deeds and glorify your Father in heaven"* (Matthew 5:16, NIV).

Ascending to new realms can also enhance our emotional resilience. With a stronger foundation in faith, we can respond to challenges with grace and strength, inspiring others to do the same. Our ability to remain calm and hopeful in tough times can encourage those struggling with anxiety and fear. A higher level of influence allows us to build stronger, more meaningful relationships. We can create an atmosphere of support and encouragement by demonstrating love, patience, and understanding. *"As iron sharpens iron, so one person sharpens another"* (Proverbs 27:17, NIV).

The vision John received in Revelation is crucial for understanding how to ascend. God wants to reveal His plans and purposes to us, guiding us as we influence our spheres. Ascending to new realms often requires letting go of old habits and mindsets. It means embracing change and being willing to adapt to new circumstances. *"See, I am doing a new thing! Now it springs up; do you not perceive it?"* (Isaiah 43:19, NIV). The more we draw near

God, the better we understand His voice and leadership.

Faith is the key that unlocks our ability to ascend and influence. When we trust God and His promises, we are empowered to take bold steps of faith. *"For just as the body without the spirit is dead, so also faith without works is dead"* (James 2:26, NIV).

As we receive God's direction, we must act on it, stepping out in confidence and courage. This can lead to unexpected opportunities for influence.

Our faith journey can inspire others to pursue their ascension. By sharing our experiences and victories, we can encourage those around us to step out of their comfort zones and into the new realms God has for them. As we ascend to new realms of influence, we must remain grounded in our faith and connected to God. This connection empowers us to impact our world positively.

With more significant influence comes greater responsibility. Jesus taught us to serve others just as He served (*Mark 10:45, NIV*). Our influence should reflect His love and grace, touching the lives of those around us. We are not meant to ascend alone. Building a community of like-minded believers can amplify our influence. We can support and uplift one another, encouraging each other to reach new heights.

Our influence is a gift from God. We must steward it wisely, using our platforms to glorify Him and advance His Kingdom. As we ascend to new realms of influence, we can create a ripple effect of positive change, inspiring others to seek God and fulfill their purpose.

CHAPTER SEVEN

THE POWER OF FAMILY IN YOUR FOCUSED LIFE

F amily plays a vital role in our lives, influencing our values, beliefs, and decisions. When striving for a focused life, understanding how our family impacts our focus and purpose is essential. Our families can either support our journey or create distractions, making it vital to cultivate a home environment that encourages focus and alignment with God's will.

Families are often our first support systems, providing emotional, spiritual, and practical support as we pursue our goals and purposes. When family members are aligned with God's vision for their lives, they can inspire and motivate one another. Family members can offer encouragement and reassurance in times of doubt or discouragement. *"Two are better than one because they have a good return for their labor: If either falls, one can help the other up"* (*Ecclesiastes 4:9-10, NIV*).

Families that set common spiritual and personal goals foster a sense of unity and purpose. This collective focus helps keep everyone accountable and committed to their paths. Families are the primary place where we learn values and principles.

The lessons taught at home shape our character and influence our ability to stay focused on our purpose. Parents and family members serve as role models. Children who see their parents actively pursuing God's purpose and demonstrating discipline are likelier to adopt similar behaviors.

A home centered on God provides the best foundation for a focused life. This involves creating an atmosphere of prayer, worship, and biblical teaching. Regular family devotions encourage spiritual growth and unity. They provide an opportunity to reflect on God's Word and how it applies to each family member's life. *"Unless the Lord builds the house, the builders labor in vain" (Psalm 127:1, NIV).*

Encouraging open dialogue about each family member's goals, challenges, and spiritual journey fosters a supportive environment. Every family faces challenges, but navigating these obstacles together can strengthen bonds and enhance focus. Difficult times often reveal the importance of support and unity. Families must learn to handle disagreements and conflicts healthily. Families can uplift one another during times of struggle through prayer and encouragement. *"Carry each other's burdens, and in this way, you will fulfill the law of Christ" (Galatians 6:2, NIV).*

While family is essential, balancing family responsibilities and individual goals is crucial. Each family member should pursue their unique purpose while supporting one another. Encourage each family member to explore their gifts and passions. When everyone is focused on their calling, the family can thrive.

Understanding the Spiritual Responsibility for Your Family

Every family has a spiritual responsibility that significantly impacts its members' lives. This responsibility encompasses nurturing faith, guiding moral values, and creating an environment that fosters spiritual growth.

As believers, we must understand and embrace this role, recognizing that our actions and decisions can influence future generations. This chapter explores the depth of spiritual responsibility within the family, emphasizing leading by example and being intentional in our spiritual journey.

Spiritual leadership in the family begins with recognizing that parents and guardians have a crucial role in shaping the spiritual lives of their children. *"These commandments that I give you today are to be on your hearts. Impress them on your children. Talk about them when you sit at home, walk along the road, lie down, and get up"* (*Deuteronomy 6:6-7, NIV*). Parents must model the faith they wish to instill in their children. Children who see their parents actively living out their faith are likelier to adopt similar beliefs and practices.

Creating a spiritual environment at home is essential for nurturing faith. This environment should be characterized by love, grace, and encouragement. Every family member has unique spiritual needs, and addressing these needs is crucial for fostering individual growth within the family unit.

Understanding each family member's spiritual journey allows for tailored support. *"From him, the whole body joined and held together by every supporting ligament, grows and builds itself up in love, as each part does its work"* (*Ephesians 4:16, NIV*).

Supporting each family member's unique spiritual interests —through service, study, or worship—can enhance their relationship with God. *"For just as each of us has one body with many members, and these members do not all have the same function, so in Christ we, though many, form one body, and each member belongs to all the others"* (*Romans 12:4-6, NIV*). Every family faces challenges, and approaching these issues from a spiritual perspective can lead to healing and growth.

Spiritual responsibility extends beyond the present; it involves leaving a lasting legacy for future generations. Families should prioritize teaching their children about faith, values, and traditions. *"We will not hide these truths from our children; we will tell the next generation about the Lord's power and the wonderful deeds he did" (Psalm 78:4, NIV).* By living out a life of integrity, love, and service, families can leave a legacy that influences their children and grandchildren.

"The righteous lead blameless lives; blessed are their children after them" (Proverbs 20:7, NIV). This encourages families to strive for righteousness, knowing it positively impacts their descendants.

How Family Challenges Can Shape Your Character

Family challenges can be complex, but they often provide valuable opportunities for personal growth and character development. These challenges can take many forms, such as conflict, loss, or emotional struggles. When approached with a spirit of resilience and faith, they can teach important lessons about ourselves and our relationships.

Facing challenges within the family can be tricky, but they can also build resilience. Just as athletes strengthen their muscles through resistance training, we can develop emotional strength through life's challenges. Romans 5:3-4 (NIV) teaches us, *"We also glory in our sufferings because we know that suffering produces perseverance; perseverance, character; and character, hope."* Each trial can help us learn how to cope and adapt, preparing us for future difficulties.

Difficult family situations often provide perspective on what truly matters. In moments of struggle, we may discover strengths we didn't know we had. This perspective helps us appreciate the good times and recognize the blessings in our lives. When we experience conflict or hardship, we learn to empathize with others facing similar situations. Sharing challenges within the family can create bonds of understanding and support.

When family members see each other's vulnerabilities, it fosters a deeper connection. Difficult times often lead us to reflect on our behavior and attitudes. When conflicts arise, we can examine our responses and make necessary changes. Lamentations 3:40

(NIV) encourages us to *"examine our ways and test them, and let us return to the Lord."* This self-reflection can lead to personal transformation.

Challenges can inspire us to set new goals for ourselves and our families. Whether it's improving communication, building trust, or prioritizing time together, these goals can lead to healthier family dynamics. Philippians 3:13-14 (NIV) encourages us to *"forget what is behind and strain toward what is ahead,"* reminding us that we can move forward with purpose.

When tensions rise within the family, patience becomes essential. Proverbs 14:29 (NIV) states, *"Whoever is patient has great understanding, but one who is quick-tempered displays folly."* Developing patience helps us navigate conflicts more calmly and thoughtfully.

Family challenges can hurt feelings, but forgiveness is crucial to healing. Ephesians 4:32 (NIV) encourages us to *"be kind and compassionate to one another, forgiving each other, just as in Christ God forgave you."* Choosing to forgive can release the burden of anger and resentment, paving the way for stronger relationships.

In times of difficulty, we may find ourselves seeking God's guidance and strength more fervently. Philippians 4:6-7 (NIV) encourages us *"not to be anxious about anything, but in every situation, by prayer and petition, with thanksgiving, present your requests to God."* Relying on God during challenging times can deepen our relationship with Him.

Family struggles can be disheartening, but remembering God has a plan for our lives brings hope. Jeremiah 29:11 (NIV) assures us that *"For I know the plans I have for you,"* declares the Lord, *"plans to prosper you and not to harm you, plans to give you hope and a future."* Trusting in God's purpose can provide comfort amidst trials.

Joseph's Dream and the Role of Family

Joseph dreams that he and his brothers are binding sheaves of grain in the field. Suddenly, his sheaf rises and stands upright while his brothers' sheaves gather around and bow down to it. This dream symbolizes Joseph's future leadership and the respect he would eventually command over his family.

In the second dream, Joseph sees the sun, moon, and eleven stars bowing to him. This dream suggests that his brothers and parents will recognize his authority and significance. This symbolism points to the future, where Joseph's position will elevate him above his family. God had a unique destiny for Joseph, unfolding through trials and triumphs.

Joseph's brothers are quick to react with jealousy and anger. They struggle with the idea of bowing down to him, feeling threatened by the prospect of his future success. This response illustrates how dreams can lead to family conflict, especially when challenging the status quo.

Jacob, Joseph's father, shows favoritism by giving Joseph a richly ornamented robe, further intensifying the brothers' resentment. This favoritism creates a divide within the family, highlighting the impact of parental favoritism on sibling relationships. As *"Hatred stirs up conflict, but love covers over all wrongs"* (Proverbs 10:12, NIV) reminds us, Joseph's family's lack of love and understanding leads to strife, emphasizing the importance of unity and support within our families.

Families can either support our dreams or create obstacles. In Joseph's case, his brothers' jealousy drives them to plot against him. This reminds us that not all family members will understand or accept our God-given dreams.

The challenges Joseph faces due to his family's reaction ultimately contribute to his growth. The conflicts within the family lead Joseph to Egypt, where he will fulfill God's plan for him. Throughout Joseph's trials, including betrayal and imprisonment, God remains sovereign. *"We know that in all things God works for the good of those who love him"* (Romans 8:28, NIV) assures us.

Joseph's faith in God's plan sustains him through complex family relationships. Joseph's unwavering faith demonstrates that even when family members do not support our dreams, we can still rely on God's guidance and purpose.

His journey exemplifies how God can transform challenges into opportunities for growth and fulfillment.

CHAPTER EIGHT

UNLOCKING YOUR FULL POTENTIAL

God has equipped each of us with unique abilities and strengths. These gifts can range from natural talents, such as artistic skills or leadership qualities, to spiritual gifts, like wisdom, faith, or healing.

To unlock your potential, taking time to assess what you do well is essential. Reflect on your past experiences, listen to feedback from others, and pay attention to what activities bring you joy and fulfillment. *"Each of you should use whatever gift you have received to serve others"* (1 Peter 4:10, NIV) emphasizes that identifying and utilizing our gifts is crucial.

Once you identify your gifts, aligning your goals with God's purpose is vital. This alignment ensures that your efforts lead to fulfillment and success. Consider how your unique gifts can be used to serve God and others. What specific goals can you set that reflect your talents and passions?

Often, we may struggle with self-doubt or limiting beliefs that hinder our progress. These negative thoughts can prevent us from stepping into our full potential. Take note of any recurring thoughts that make you feel unworthy or incapable. Challenge these beliefs by comparing them with what God says about you.

Challenges and setbacks are an inevitable part of life, but they can also be valuable growth opportunities. When faced with difficulties, it's essential to maintain a positive perspective and seek God's guidance. Instead of viewing challenges as roadblocks, consider them lessons that help you grow and develop resilience.

Unlocking your divine potential requires action. Recognizing your gifts and setting goals is not enough; you must actively pursue them.

How to Interpret Your Life's Purpose in Light of God's Kingdom

Understanding your life's purpose can feel daunting, but viewing it through the lens of God's Kingdom brings clarity. God's Kingdom represents His will, values, and plans for humanity. Aligning your purpose with this greater Kingdom perspective reveals a deeper meaning and fosters a fulfilling relationship with God.

The first step is to seek God's will through prayer, Scripture, and openness to His leading. God has equipped us with unique gifts and talents that reflect His character and contribute to His Kingdom's expansion. Evaluate your strengths, passions, and experiences. Reflect on what you enjoy doing and feel called to do.

1 Corinthians 12:4-7 (NIV) teaches us that *"There are different kinds of gifts, but the same Spirit distributes them. The manifestation of the Spirit is given to each one for the common good."* Recognizing your gifts is crucial to understanding your purpose.

Every believer's fundamental purpose is to share the Gospel and make disciples, aligning personal purpose with God's greater mission. Consider spreading Christ's message through personal relationships, community service, or church activities.

God's Kingdom is built on relationships and community. Understanding your role within the body of Christ is essential. Engage with your church community and seek ways to serve.

Interpreting your life's purpose in light of God's Kingdom

means embodying Kingdom values like love, service, justice, and humility. Make a conscious effort to reflect these values in your interactions. *"He has shown you, O mortal, what is good. And what does the Lord require of you? To act justly and to love mercy and to walk humbly with your God"* (Micah 6:8, NIV) reminds us.

Trust in God's unique timing for your purpose. Sometimes, the path may not be clear, but trusting in His timing allows growth and preparation. Develop patience, knowing God's plan unfolds at the right time. Use this waiting period to deepen your relationship with Him. As *"For everything, there is a season, and a time for every matter under heaven"* (Ecclesiastes 3:1, NIV), assures us.

Seeing the Future Through God's Perspective

We often find ourselves consumed by worries about what lies ahead, whether in our personal lives, careers, or broader societal issues. However, as believers, we can take comfort that God sees the future in its entirety.

A powerful example of this is found in the story of Daniel, particularly in Daniel 2:1 (NIV), where we see God revealing His plans through visions and dreams. *"In the second year of his reign, Nebuchadnezzar had dreams; his spirit was troubled, and his sleep left him."* This moment occurred during the reign of King Nebuchadnezzar of Babylon, who was troubled by dreams he couldn't understand.

King Nebuchadnezzar, not a believer in God, experienced anxiety over his dreams, showing that even those outside of faith can feel the weight of the unknown. In the ancient world, dreams were often viewed as significant messages from the divine. God chose to use Nebuchadnezzar's dreams to reveal future events, indicating His control over the kingdoms of men.

As Proverbs 19:21 (NIV) reminds us, *"Many are the plans in the mind of a man, but it is the purpose of the Lord that will stand."* In moments of uncertainty, seeking God's perspective is essential.

Daniel, a servant of God, exemplified this by turning to prayer and seeking understanding from the Lord. The revelation of the king's dream provides insight into God's overarching plans. The dream illustrated the rise and fall of kingdoms, demonstrating God's active involvement in shaping history.

The dream revealed a statue representing different empires, ultimately showing God's kingdom would stand forever. This assures us that God's purpose remains despite earthly powers and uncertainties. As *"Declaring the end from the beginning, and from ancient times things not yet done"* (Isaiah 46:10, NIV) emphasizes.

Understanding that God sees the future allows us to face uncertainty with faith. Just as He revealed His plans to Daniel, He can guide us in our own lives. We can replace fear and anxiety with peace when we trust God's perspective.

This trust enables us to move forward, knowing God has a plan for us.

How to Respond to God's Calling Like David

David's story begins in 1 Samuel 16, where God instructs Samuel to anoint David as king while still a shepherd. This demonstrates that God often calls us when we least expect it and may not seem qualified in the world's eyes.

To respond to God's calling, we must recognize His voice amid life's noise. As *"My sheep hear my voice, and I know them, and they follow me"* (John 10:27, NIV) indicates, growing closer to God makes us more adept at hearing His call.

Before becoming king, David served as a shepherd, caring for his father's sheep. This period taught him humility, patience, and hard work, and David's dedication prepared him for greater responsibilities. Like David, we must be faithful in our current roles, no matter how small. As Luke 16:10 reminds us, "One who is faithful in a very little is also faithful in much" (NIV).

David's encounter with Goliath (1 Samuel 17) shows that stepping out in faith is essential. David relied on his faith to defeat the giant. We must trust God equips us to face challenges and take action based on faith.

Throughout his life, David sought God's guidance. He inquired of the Lord before battle (1 Samuel 30:8). This habit ensured wise choices and alignment with God's plans.

David faced challenges, including betrayal, loss, and moral failures. Each experience shaped him into a king after God's heart. Responding to God's call often involves perseverance through trials.

David led with compassion, seeking to serve rather than be served. Responding to God's calling involves leadership with integrity, love, and humility. As *"Shepherd the flock of God that is among you, exercising oversight, not under compulsion, but willingly, as God would have you"* (1 Peter 5:2-3, NIV), encourages. Authentic leadership reflects God's character.

CHAPTER NINE

FOCUSED RELATIONSHIPS: LEADING LOVED ONES TO GOD

T he foundation of any strong relationship is love. The Bible tells us that "God is love" (1 John 4:8, NIV). We must demonstrate love in our interactions to lead our loved ones to Him.

Show your loved ones that you care for them without conditions, mirroring God's love as *"A new commandment I give to you, that you love one another: just as I have loved you, you also are to love one another. By this, all people will know that you are my disciples if you have a love for one another"* (John 13:34-35, ESV), emphasizes.

Effective communication is critical. Encourage open conversations about faith and spiritual matters. Engage your loved ones with open-ended questions. Proverbs 18:13 (NIV) warns, *"If one answers before he hears, it is his folly and shame."* Listening first fosters understanding and connection.

Sharing your personal faith journey can impact your loved ones. Be open about struggles and victories. Authenticity is powerful.

Let your loved ones see how God has worked in your life. Revelation 12:11 (NIV) reminds us, *"And they have conquered him by the blood of the Lamb and by the word of their testimony."* Your story can inspire others.

Your actions speak louder than words. Show your loved ones what it means to live a life focused on Christ. Display the fruits of the Spirit (*"the fruit of the Spirit is love, joy, peace, patience, kindness, goodness, faithfulness, gentleness, self-control"*; Galatians 5:22-23, NIV) in your daily life.

"In the same way, let your light shine before others, so that they may see your good works and give glory to your Father who is in heaven" (Matthew 5:16, ESV) encourages.

Cultivate an environment nurturing spiritual growth. Participate in church activities, Bible studies, or volunteer work together. Hebrews 10:24-25 (NIV) exhorts, *"And let us consider how to stir up one another to love and good works, not neglecting to meet together, as is the habit of some, but encouraging one another."*

Remember, every faith journey is unique. Be patient with your loved ones. Encourage positive movement toward faith. Every step matters. Trust *"that he who began a good work in you will bring it to completion on the day of Jesus Christ"* (Philippians 1:6, NIV).

The Role of Relationships in Your Spiritual Journey

God designed us for relationships. In Ecclesiastes 4:9-10, the Bible states, *"Two are better than one because they have a good reward for their toil. For if they fall, one will lift up his fellow."* (ESV) Being part of a community can give us the support and encouragement needed to navigate our spiritual paths.

When we share our experiences with others, we learn and grow together. A community of believers can offer insights, wisdom, and understanding that enrich our spiritual lives. Hebrews 10:24-25 *"stir up one another to love and good works, not neglecting to meet together."* (NIV) Regular fellowship helps keep our focus on

God and fosters deeper connections.

Having an accountability partner can be a powerful asset in our spiritual journeys. This person can help us focus on our goals and encourage us in our walk with God. Discussing spiritual goals with someone you trust can keep you motivated. Whether praying daily, reading Scripture or serving in the community, having someone to check in with helps maintain focus. Proverbs 27:17 says, *"Iron sharpens iron, and one man sharpens another."* (NIV) Encouragement and constructive feedback from others can help us grow and develop our faith.

Mentorship is another vital aspect of relationships in our spiritual journeys. Learning from someone more experienced can provide guidance and wisdom. Find a mentor who can offer biblical wisdom and support. Their experiences and understanding can help you navigate challenges and deepen your faith.

Family is often the first place we encounter faith. The relationships we build within our families can profoundly influence our spiritual development. Encourage family discussions about religion, prayer, and the Bible. Create a home where everyone feels comfortable exploring their beliefs and asking questions. Deuteronomy 6:6-7 instructs us to talk about God's commandments: *"when you sit in your house, and when you walk by the way, and when you lie down, and when you rise."* (ESV) Integrating faith into daily life strengthens family bonds and deepens everyone's understanding of God.

In our spiritual journeys, we will face challenges and struggles. Relationships provide the support needed to overcome these obstacles. Offer a listening ear or a helping hand to those in need. Being present in someone's life can significantly impact their faith journey, reminding them of God's love and care.

Relationships are not always easy. Conflicts and disagreements can arise and lead to personal and spiritual growth. Approach conflicts with grace and a willingness to understand the other person's perspective. These experiences can teach us about humility, forgiveness, and patience. Matthew 18:15-17 guides resolving conflicts within the community, emphasizing the importance of reconciliation and maintaining unity.

Relationships can either draw us closer to God or lead us away from His plans for our lives. The first step to aligning relationships with God's purpose is ensuring our connections are rooted in faith. When both parties share similar beliefs and values, it creates a strong foundation for growth.

Healthy communication is crucial to any relationship. Discussing your thoughts, feelings, and spiritual journeys can help you maintain alignment with God's purpose. Talk about your dreams and aspirations and how they align with God's purpose for your lives. Encourage each other to pursue these goals.

No relationship is perfect, and conflicts are bound to arise. Practicing forgiveness is crucial in keeping relationships aligned with God's purpose. Holding onto bitterness can damage relationships. Make a conscious effort to forgive and move forward.

Help one another grow in your relationship with God. This support can take many forms, such as prayer, studying Scripture, or attending church events together. Encourage one another to pursue personal growth in faith.

Serving others as a team can strengthen your relationship and align it with God's purpose. It fosters a sense of unity and shared mission. Find opportunities to serve in your community or church. Working together towards a common goal can deepen your bond.

Establishing healthy boundaries helps maintain focus on God's purpose. It ensures that relationships don't become sources of distraction or compromise your values. Make sure your relationships do not overshadow your relationship with God. Keep a balance between spending time with loved ones and nurturing your spiritual life. 1 Corinthians 10:23 reminds us that *while all things may be permissible, not all things are beneficial.* (NIV) Setting boundaries helps you prioritize what truly matters.

Love and respect are foundational elements in any relationship. Cultivating these qualities helps maintain alignment with God's purpose. Regularly express gratitude for one another. Acknowledging each other's efforts fosters a positive atmosphere. 1 Peter 4:8 tells us to *love one another deeply, for love covers a multitude of sins.* (NIV) A strong foundation of love helps relationships thrive despite challenges

CHAPTER TEN

RISING ABOVE CHAOS AND OPPOSITION

C haos refers to times when things seem out of control. It could be when your plans fall apart, your relationships get complicated, or unexpected problems arise. Conversely, opposition involves people or situations that actively stand in the way of your progress, purpose, or spiritual growth. This could be through conflict, criticism, or obstacles that make moving forward difficult.

The Bible gives plenty of examples of people who faced chaos and opposition yet overcame it because they trusted God's plan. David, for instance, faced opposition from King Saul, who sought to kill him out of jealousy. Despite the chaos of running for his life and living in exile, David kept his trust in God. He rose above the chaos by holding onto God's promises and eventually became king as God had intended (1 Samuel 16-24).

When we rise above chaos and opposition, we are not allowing circumstances or people to dictate our faith or purpose. Rising above means we focus on God's calling, knowing that opposition is temporary, but God's plan for our lives is eternal. *"But those who hope in the Lord will renew their strength. They will soar on wings like eagles; they will run and not grow weary; they will walk and not be faint"* (Isaiah 40:31, NIV). This verse reminds us that our strength to rise above the chaos comes from hoping in the Lord.

The key to rising above is faith. Faith allows us to see beyond the chaos and opposition, trusting that God is working everything together for our good. Even when life feels out of control, God is still in control. *"God is our refuge and strength, an ever-present help in trouble"* (Psalm 46:1, NIV). When we face opposition or chaos, we can find refuge in God, trusting He is sovereign and has a plan to bring us through it.

It's easy to focus on the negative when faced with opposition, but keeping a Kingdom perspective helps us see beyond our immediate problems. *"Set your minds on things above, not earthly things"* (Colossians 3:2, NIV). This means focusing on God's eternal promises rather than getting lost in life's temporary struggles.

Jesus is the ultimate example of someone who faced constant opposition but rose with grace and purpose above it all. From the moment He began His ministry, Jesus encountered resistance —from religious leaders, doubters, and even Satan himself. Yet, He remained focused on His mission, never allowing the chaos around Him to distract Him from His purpose.

In Matthew 4:1-11, when Satan tempted Jesus in the wilderness, He overcame by standing firm on God's Word. He responded to every temptation with Scripture, rising above Satan's schemes by focusing on God's truth. Later, in the Garden of Gethsemane (Matthew 26:36-46), when Jesus was under immense pressure before His crucifixion, He turned to prayer. Through prayer, He aligned His will with God's, empowering Him to face the cross with courage and resolve.

If Jesus, the Son of God, faced opposition and chaos but overcame it through faith, prayer, and trust in God's plan, we can rise above whatever we face in life.

God's Word is our foundation in times of chaos and opposition. *"Your word is a lamp for my feet, a light on my path"* (Psalm 119:105, NIV). When rooted in the Bible, we find guidance, strength, and wisdom to navigate even the most difficult situations.

In the story of Peter walking on water (Matthew 14:22-33), Peter could do the impossible as long as he kept his eyes on Jesus. But he began to sink when he focused on the wind and the waves (the chaos around him). Similarly, we must keep our eyes on Jesus, the source of our strength, to rise above our challenges.

Opposition can often make us feel discouraged or question our purpose. But opposition is a sign that we are on the right path. Rising above chaos and opposition requires persistence. *"Let us not become weary in doing good, for at the proper time we will reap a harvest if we do not give up"* (Galatians 6:9, NIV). Keep pressing forward, knowing that God will reward your persistence and faith.

God promises that when we rise above chaos and opposition, we will overcome and experience growth, strength, and a more profound purpose. When we rise above life's challenges, we reflect God's strength and character to those around us. Our perseverance becomes a testimony of His faithfulness, inspiring others to trust Him, even in their battles.

Turning Chaos into Purposeful Action

Life is full of challenges, and often, things don't go as planned. Whether it's unexpected circumstances, personal struggles, or external forces, chaos can make us feel overwhelmed and confused. But in the middle of the mess, God can still bring order, direction, and purpose. He specializes in turning chaos into purposeful action, using even the difficult moments in our lives to accomplish His more excellent plan.

Chaos can take many forms—disruptions at work, family problems, financial troubles, health issues, or emotional turmoil. Sometimes, it results from things beyond our control, and other times, it results from our own decisions.

The Bible gives examples of people who faced chaotic situations but allowed God to turn them around for good. Joseph was sold into slavery by his brothers. His life seemed to spiral into chaos as he faced betrayal, false accusations, and imprisonment. But even amid all that confusion, God had a plan. Joseph's time in Egypt was part of God's greater purpose to save his family and many others during a severe famine (Genesis 50:20).

Just like Joseph, we may not always see God's plan when things seem out of control. But we can trust that God is working behind the scenes, turning what looks like chaos into something meaningful. From the beginning, God has shown His ability to bring order out of chaos.

In Genesis 1, the earth was formless and empty, but God spoke, and everything came into being. *"For God is not a God of disorder but of peace"* (1 Corinthians 14:33, NIV). This means that God's nature is to create order, and we can trust Him to do that in our lives.

No matter how confusing or overwhelming things seem, God can bring peace and purpose to any situation.

One of the most potent ways God works is by taking the broken pieces of our lives and turning them into something beautiful. God sees what we see as chaos as an opportunity for transformation and growth.

Let's allow God to turn our chaos into purposeful action. Trusting God's plan is critical even when life doesn't make sense. While there are many things in life that we can't control, we can always choose how we respond. Amid the chaos, it's essential to focus on what is within our control—our attitude, our faith, and our actions. *"Do not be anxious about anything, but in every situation, by prayer and petition, with thanksgiving, present your requests to God. And the peace of God, which transcends all understanding, will guard your hearts and your minds in Christ Jesus"* (Philippians 4:6-7, NIV).

Instead of being paralyzed by confusion, we can start taking small, intentional steps toward order. In times of chaos, it's easy to feel we must fix everything at once. But often, God calls us to do the next right thing simply. *"The Lord makes firm the steps of the one who delights in him"* (Psalm 37:23, NIV).

Chaos is uncomfortable, but it's also an opportunity for growth. Every challenging situation we face can teach us something valuable. *"Suffering produces perseverance; perseverance, character; and character, hope"* (Romans 5:3-4, NIV).

Moses and the Israelites found themselves trapped between the Red Sea and the Egyptian army. It was a chaotic and hopeless situation, but God parted the sea, allowing them to escape. What seemed like chaos became an opportunity for God to show His power and deliver His people.

Throughout his ministry, Paul faced many trials—imprisonment, shipwrecks, beatings, and more. Yet, amid all this chaos, Paul continued to preach the Gospel and write letters that would become part of the New Testament. *"My grace is sufficient for you, for my power is made perfect in weakness"* (2 Corinthians 12:9, NIV).

God used Paul's challenging circumstances to advance His Kingdom in ways Paul couldn't have imagined.

Perhaps the ultimate example of God turning chaos into purpose is Jesus' crucifixion. What looked like the ultimate defeat—Jesus' death on the cross—became the most significant victory. Through His death and resurrection, Jesus brought salvation to the world.

Stepping into Destiny Amid Overflowing Rivers

The Israelites, led by Joshua, had wandered in the wilderness for 40 years. They were now on the brink of entering the Promised Land, but there was a significant challenge in front of them: the Jordan River was overflowing its banks during harvest season. The river represented a barrier between them and their destiny, and crossing it seemed impossible from a human perspective.

Joshua 3:13-15 *"As soon as the priests who carry the ark of the Lord —the Lord of all the earth—set foot in the Jordan, its waters flowing downstream will be cut off and stand up in a heap. So when the people broke camp to cross the Jordan, the priests carrying the ark of the covenant went ahead of them. Now the Jordan is at flood stage all during harvest, yet as soon as the priests who carried the ark reached the Jordan and their feet touched the water's edge, the water from upstream stopped flowing."* (NIV)

The Israelites did not cross the Jordan when the river was calm. Instead, they arrived when the river was at its highest point—flood season. From a natural perspective, this seemed like the worst possible time to cross, yet it was God's chosen time.

This teaches us that stepping into our destiny doesn't always happen when everything looks easy or convenient. Sometimes, God allows us to face seemingly insurmountable challenges to demonstrate His power. Like the Israelites, you may feel like you're facing your "Jordan" at its most impossible point, but that's often when God's timing is perfect.

Isaiah 55:8-9 reminds us, *"For my thoughts are not your thoughts, neither are your ways my ways," declares the Lord. "As the heavens are higher than the earth, so are my ways higher than your ways and my thoughts than your thoughts."* (NIV) God's ways are higher than ours, and His timing, though it may not align with our expectations, is always right.

Notice that the waters of the Jordan didn't stop flowing until the priests stepped into the river. They had to act in faith before they saw the miracle. God didn't part the waters until the priests carrying the ark put their feet in it. This was a significant act of faith, especially considering the river was at flood stage.

Hebrews 11:1 says, *"Now faith is confidence in what we hope for and assurance about what we do not see"* (NIV). *Even when we can't see the whole picture, acting in faith is critical to* moving toward our God-given destiny.

The ark of the covenant, which symbolized God's presence, went ahead of the people. The priests carrying the ark stepped into the river first, representing God's leadership and presence before the Israelites entered their challenge.

In our own lives, we must recognize that we don't face challenges or step into destiny alone. God goes before us. When stepping into the unknown or facing overwhelming obstacles, remember that God is already ahead of you, preparing the way. Deuteronomy 31:8 reassures us that *"The Lord himself goes before you and will be with you; he will never leave you nor forsake you."* (NIV)

Knowing that God is leading the way gives us the courage to take bold steps of faith.

The Jordan River, at flood stage, was a significant obstacle. From a natural perspective, it should have stopped the Israelites in their tracks. Yet, no obstacle can prevent His plan from unfolding when God is involved.

In your journey toward fulfilling your destiny, you will face "Jordan Rivers"—obstacles that seem impossible to overcome. But just as God stopped the waters of the Jordan, He can remove or reduce the challenges in your life when you move forward in faith.

Isaiah 43:16 reminds us, *"This is what the Lord says—he who made a way through the sea, a path through the mighty waters."* (NIV) No matter how significant, obstacles cannot stop God's purposes when you trust Him and step out in faith.

God had promised the Israelites the land of Canaan. Their trust in His promise was essential in overcoming their fear of the Jordan River. They believed that God would do what He said, even though the circumstances looked impossible.

In your life, stepping into destiny means standing on God's promises. When He says He has a plan for your life or will never leave or forsake you, you can trust those promises, no matter what obstacles stand in your way.

Trusting in God's promises enables you to keep moving forward, even when you don't see how everything will work out.

The priests who carried the ark into the river were taking a step of faith, but their actions impacted the entire nation. Because of their obedience, the waters were stopped, and all the Israelites crossed into the Promised Land on dry ground. Your steps of faith aren't just for you—they can impact the lives of others around you. Your family, friends, or community may be waiting for you to take that step of faith that God calls you to. Like the priests, your obedience can lead others to their breakthroughs. Matthew 5:16 encourages us to let our light shine before others so that they may see our good deeds and glorify God.

CHAPTER ELEVEN

LIVING FOR ETERNITY: UNDERSTANDING ETERNAL FOCUS

L iving for the Kingdom of God means making His will, values, and purposes the central focus of your life. It's about aligning every aspect of your decisions, priorities, relationships, and actions with advancing God's Kingdom on earth.

When you choose to live for the Kingdom, you prioritize what is eternal over what is temporary, finding true purpose and fulfillment in doing what God has called you to do. Living for the Kingdom involves following the teachings of Jesus Christ, seeking God's direction in all things, and allowing His Word to shape your life.

"But seek first the Kingdom of God and His righteousness, and all these things will be given to you as well" (Matthew 6:33, NIV). This verse shows us that everything else falls into place when we make God's Kingdom our primary focus.

You seek to do what God desires, even when difficult or countercultural. This means submitting your plans, ambitions, and desires to God and trusting His perfect will.

Instead of chasing after material things, fame, or worldly success, you focus on building a relationship with God and making a positive impact that will last beyond this life. You strive to live a holy life, reflecting Christ in your actions, thoughts, and words.

You become a vessel for God's purposes, whether by sharing the gospel, serving others, or living a life that points people to Jesus.

When you live for the Kingdom, you build a legacy that will have an eternal impact. The things of this world are temporary, but the fruit of a life lived for God lasts forever.

"Set your minds on things above, not on earthly things" (Colossians 3:2, NIV), encouraging us to keep our eyes on eternal rewards rather than the fleeting pleasures of this world.

When you live for God, your faithfulness, love, and obedience to His Word influence those around you—whether it's your family, friends, or community, you become a living testimony of God's goodness.

Every act of kindness, every prayer, every sacrifice made for the Kingdom has a ripple effect. The spiritual seeds you plant today can bear fruit long after you're gone, affecting future generations.

Scripture speaks of crowns and rewards that await believers who live faithfully for God (see 2 Timothy 4:8). Living for the Kingdom ensures that your efforts are not in vain; your life is making an eternal difference.

Jesus said, *"The Son of Man did not come to be served, but to serve, and to give his life as a ransom for many"* (Mark 10:45, NIV).

When you serve others, you are living out Kingdom values, showing the love of Christ to those in need. Serving selflessly also draws you closer to God and deepens your understanding of His heart.

It's easy to get caught up in the busyness of life, but remember that living for the Kingdom requires an eternal perspective. Regularly remind yourself that the things of this world are temporary and your true treasure is in heaven.

This mindset helps you make decisions based on eternal significance, not just immediate gratification.

Living for the Kingdom doesn't happen in isolation. Surround yourself with other believers who are encouraging you to pursue God's will and live out your faith.

Together, you can strengthen each other and work to advance God's Kingdom in your communities.

Living for the Kingdom isn't always easy. It may involve sacrifices, challenges, and even opposition from the world.

But Jesus promises that those who endure will be rewarded. *"Blessed are those who are persecuted because of righteousness, for theirs is the Kingdom of heaven"* (Matthew 5:10, NIV).

You will face moments when the world's values clash with Kingdom values.

In those moments, staying grounded in prayer and Scripture is necessary, drawing strength from God to remain focused on His mission.

One of the most profound effects of living for the Kingdom is your lasting legacy for future generations.

Living for God's purposes creates a foundation for those who come after you to know and experience His love.

"We will not hide them from their descendants; we will tell the next generation the praiseworthy deeds of the Lord, his power, and the wonders he has done" (Psalm 78:4, NIV).

When you live for the Kingdom, you help shape the next generation's faith by sharing God's work in your life and modeling a life devoted to Him.

Why Living for God's Kingdom Shapes Your Legacy

Living for God's Kingdom is not just about the present moment —it's about building something that lasts beyond your lifetime. Committing to serving God and pursuing His purposes leaves a spiritual legacy that can impact future generations.

This legacy is shaped not by material success or temporary achievements but by a life with eternal values anchored in faith, love, and obedience to God. Most of what we achieve in life fades over time—wealth can be spent, titles can be forgotten, and possessions can be lost.

However, when you live for God's Kingdom, your life leaves an eternal impact. *"Do not store up for yourselves treasures on earth, where moth and rust destroy, and where thieves break in and steal. But store up for yourselves treasures in heaven, where moth and rust do not destroy, and where thieves do not break in and steal"* (Matthew 6:19-20, NIV).

These treasures are eternal: the relationships you foster in Christ, the souls you bring to the Lord, and the acts of kindness and love you do for others in His name.

Living for God's Kingdom ensures that your efforts go beyond the here and now, making a difference in eternity. This spiritual investment leaves a legacy of faith and service, which continues to influence you even after you're gone.

Living for the Kingdom means passing on spiritual values to those around you, particularly your family. When you live a life focused on God's principles, you actively shape the next generation's beliefs, values, and lives.

Your faith can inspire your children, grandchildren, and others around you to seek God and live for Him. The lessons they will carry forward are how you live out your faith in difficult situations, love and forgive others and serve in God's Kingdom.

This forms a robust spiritual heritage that continues to ripple through future generations. One of the greatest legacies you can leave is a life that points others to Jesus.

When you live for God's Kingdom, your actions reflect His love, grace, and mercy. Your faith becomes a testimony to God's goodness and faithfulness in your life, encouraging others to trust Him.

Just like the heroes of faith in *Hebrews 11*, your life can become a testament to what God can do through someone committed to His purposes.

When you live for the Kingdom, you align with God's purpose for your life. *"For I know the plans I have for you," declares the Lord, "plans to prosper you and not to harm you, plans to give you hope and a future"* (Jeremiah 29:11, NIV).

By seeking and fulfilling God's will, you leave behind a legacy of obedience and trust.

This legacy shows others that following God's plan leads to a life of significance, purpose, and impact.

God's Kingdom is eternal, and when you live according to His purpose, your life becomes a part of that plan.

Your work for God, whether in ministry, service, or everyday life, contributes to His greater mission.

Living for the Kingdom is not just about personal achievements; it's about serving others in love.

"For even the Son of Man did not come to be served, but to serve" (Mark 10:45, NIV).

When you adopt a servant's heart and live for others, you leave a legacy of love and compassion.

The people you help, the lives you touch, and the kindness you show will be remembered far longer than any material success.

Your legacy of love and service reflects God's heart and demonstrates what it means to be a follower of Christ.

This legacy encourages others to live selflessly and to serve those around them, continuing the cycle of Kingdom-focused living.

God's Kingdom is everlasting, and when you live for His Kingdom, your life aligns with something far more significant than yourself.

When you live for God's Kingdom, you are part of His eternal plan of redemption and restoration.

Every choice you make, every person you touch, and every action you take in alignment with God's will has a purpose that extends into eternity.

This creates a legacy that cannot be measured in earthly terms but is recorded in heaven.

Living for the Kingdom of God gives you hope that surpasses this world.

"May the God of hope fill you with all joy and peace as you trust in him, so that you may overflow with hope by the power of the Holy Spirit" (Romans 15:13, NIV).

This hope, rooted in Christ, is contagious.

When others see you living with hope and faith despite challenges, they are inspired to find that same hope in Jesus.

Your legacy is not just about the impact you make during your lifetime but about the hope you instill in others to keep trusting God, even after you're gone. Based on God's promises and the assurance of eternal life, this hope leaves a lasting imprint on the hearts of those who know you.

Turning Evil into Good for God's Glory

"You intended to harm me, but God intended it for good to accomplish what is now being done, the saving of many lives." (Genesis 50:20, NIV)

When Joseph finally became second-in-command in Egypt and saved many lives during a famine, it became clear that what was meant for evil against him was used by God for good.

This story teaches us that no matter what we face—betrayal, rejection, or suffering—God can turn it all around for His glory and our good.

One of the most reassuring aspects of Joseph's story is how it demonstrates God's sovereignty.

Even when people intend to harm you or circumstances seem beyond repair, God is always in control.

Nothing surprises Him or catches Him off guard.

He can take even the evil actions of others and use them for His divine purposes.

Like Joseph, we may not always understand why things happen the way they do, but we can trust that God is working behind the scenes to bring about His will.

This gives us hope, knowing that no situation is too difficult for God to redeem.

Joseph's faith is a powerful example of what it means to trust God amid adversity.

Despite his many hardships, Joseph never lost faith in God's plan.

He endured years of suffering without knowing the complete picture, yet he trusted that God was with him every step of the way.

In our own lives, we may face seasons where it seems like everything is going wrong.

We may feel betrayed by others, abandoned, or misunderstood.

But like Joseph, we are called to trust God's timing and ability to turn things around for our good.

"For my thoughts are not your thoughts, neither are your ways my ways," declares the Lord. "As the heavens are higher than the earth,

so are my ways higher than your ways and my thoughts than your thoughts." (Isaiah 55:8-9, NIV)

What may seem like a setback or a tragedy in our eyes could be part of God's more excellent plan for our lives.

Joseph's story is not just about how God turns evil into good but also about forgiveness and restoration. Despite the terrible things his brothers did to him, Joseph chose to forgive them.

He recognized that holding on to bitterness and resentment would only hinder God's greater purpose for his life. Forgiving can be challenging when we face betrayal or hurt from others.

However, forgiveness is essential for healing and allowing God to work through us.

"Be kind and compassionate to one another, forgiving each other, just as in Christ God forgave you." (Ephesians 4:32, NIV)

By forgiving those who wrong us, we free ourselves from bitterness and allow God to restore our lives. His life shows how God can redeem even the worst situations for His glory.

In the same way, that Joseph's suffering saved many lives, God can use our struggles and trials to impact others and bring glory to His name.

Sometimes, the pain we experience becomes a platform for us to minister to others facing similar challenges. God never wastes a hurt—He uses it to shape, grow, and prepare us for His purpose for our lives.

When we surrender our pain to God, He can turn it into something beautiful that reflects His grace and power. Joseph's story shows that God's purpose will always prevail no matter what the enemy tries to do.

What others meant for harm, God turned into a blessing. This is a reminder that we, too, have a purpose that cannot be thwarted by the schemes of the enemy or the actions of others.

As long as we stay focused on God and trust in His plan, He will guide us through every trial and bring us to victory.

When we look at life's challenges, we must remember that God sees the bigger picture. He knows how everything will turn out in the end, and He has promised that His plans for us are good.

"For I know the plans I have for you," declares the Lord, "plans to prosper you and not to harm you, plans to give you hope and a future." (Jeremiah 29:11, NIV)

Joseph's story leaves a legacy of faith, perseverance, and trust in God's plan. His life teaches us that God is always at work, even when we can't see it, and that He can use any situation—no matter how difficult or painful—for His glory. By trusting God through our trials, we can leave a legacy of faith that inspires others.

Our ability to forgive, to trust in God's timing, and to see His hand at work during our challenges will encourage those around us to put their faith in God as well.

Aligning Your Resources with God's Kingdom

Stewardship is the foundation of aligning your resources with God's Kingdom. It means recognizing that everything you have comes from God, and you are called to manage it for His glory.

"The earth is the Lord's, and everything in it, the world, and all who live in it" (Psalm 24:1, NIV). This verse shows us that nothing truly belongs to us; we are caretakers of what God has given.

In the parable of the Talents recorded in Matthew 25:14-30, Jesus illustrates the importance of wisely using what God has entrusted to us. Those who were faithful with their resources were praised and rewarded, while those who failed to use their talents for God's purposes missed out on the opportunity to please God and multiply their resources.

This parable highlights the importance of active stewards, using all we have for God's Kingdom. When we make God's Kingdom our focus, He promises to provide for our needs.

Aligning your resources with God's Kingdom requires shifting your focus from self-centered to Christ-centered. Instead of asking, "How can I use my resources for my benefit?" the question becomes, "How can I use my resources to serve God and others?"

This mindset transforms how you approach your time, money, abilities, and relationships. Time is one of the most valuable resources God has given you, and how you spend it reflects your priorities.

"Be very careful, then, how you live—not as unwise but as wise, making the most of every opportunity, because the days are evil" (Ephesians 5:15-16, NIV).

This verse encourages us to make the most of our time and to use it wisely for God's purposes. To align your time with God's Kingdom, consider how much you dedicate to activities that further His will.

Are you praying, reading His Word, serving others, and sharing the gospel?

When you dedicate your time to God, you invest in things with eternal value. God has gifted each person with unique abilities and talents that can be used to build His Kingdom.

Whether your talents are in teaching, music, leadership, or serving others, these gifts are meant to glorify God and bless those around you. By using your talents for God, you demonstrate your faithfulness and bring honor to Him.

Whether you're serving in church, helping in your community, or simply encouraging others with your gifts, each act of service aligns your talents with God's purposes.

Money and material resources are often seen as personal assets, but the Bible teaches that they are tools God has given us to further His Kingdom.

"Honor the Lord with your wealth, with the first fruits of all your crops" (Proverbs 3:9, NIV).

This principle of giving back to God what He has blessed us with is a way of recognizing His provision and trusting Him to provide for our needs. Tithing, offerings, and generosity are ways to align your finances with God's Kingdom.

"Bring the whole tithe into the storehouse, that there may be food in my house. Test me in this," says the Lord Almighty, "and see if I will not throw open the floodgates of heaven and pour out so much blessing that there will not be room enough to store it" (Malachi 3:10, NIV).

When you give to God's work—whether supporting your church, missionaries, or those in need—you invest in eternal things that matter to God. Generosity is not just about giving money; it's about a heart posture that trusts God as the ultimate provider and seeks to use what He has given to bless others.

Our relationships are another vital resource that can be aligned with God's Kingdom. The people in our lives—family, friends, coworkers—are opportunities to reflect Christ's love and encourage one another toward godliness.

"Consider how we may spur one another on toward love and good deeds, not giving up meeting together...but encouraging one another" (Hebrews 10:24-25, NIV).

When we invest time in building Christ-centered relationships, we help others grow in their faith and align their resources with God's purposes.

These relationships also provide support and accountability, helping you stay focused on God's Kingdom even when distractions arise. The resources we invest in God's Kingdom have eternal consequences.

"Do not store up for yourselves treasures on earth... But store up for yourselves treasures in heaven, where moths and vermin do not destroy, and where thieves do not break in and steal" (Matthew 6:19-20, NIV).

This verse reminds us that earthly possessions and

accomplishments will one day fade away, but what we invest in God's Kingdom will last forever. When you align your resources with God's purposes, you store treasures in heaven. Every act of kindness, every offering, and every moment spent in prayer and service contributes to God's eternal plan.

The impact of aligning your resources with God's Kingdom is seen not only in this life but also in eternity. Aligning your resources with God's Kingdom means living with an eternal perspective. Instead of focusing on temporary goals, you focus on what will last forever—God's Kingdom, His glory, and the lives of people. Colossians 3:2 says, "Set your minds on things above, not earthly things."

This perspective keeps you grounded in what truly matters and helps you make decisions that honor God. When your time, talents, finances, and relationships align with God's Kingdom, you experience the joy of knowing that your life contributes to something far more significant than yourself. You are part of God's plan to transform the world and bring others into His eternal Kingdom.

CHAPTER TWELVE

FULFILLING YOUR DESTINY THROUGH SPIRITUAL ALIGNMENT

Spiritual alignment aligns your heart, mind, and spirit with God's ways. It begins with a relationship with God through Jesus Christ and grows as you seek His guidance, surrender your will, and obey His commands.

"Trust in the Lord with all your heart and lean not on your understanding; in all your ways submit to Him, and He will make your paths straight" (Proverbs 3:5-6, NIV).

When you align your life with God's direction, you begin to walk the path He has set for you, which leads to fulfilling your destiny.

In this alignment, you are not just following a set of rules but cultivating a deeper connection with God that helps you understand His will and walk in step with His Spirit.

"Do not conform to the pattern of this world, but be transformed by the renewing of your mind. Then you will be able to test and approve what God's will is—His good, pleasing, and perfect will" (Romans 12:2, NIV).

Every person has a unique destiny given by God, but fulfilling that destiny requires knowing what it is. This discovery process often involves prayer, seeking God's will, and listening to His voice through His Word and the guidance of the Holy Spirit.

Your purpose may be revealed as you faithfully follow God's leading. Sometimes, it may come through life experiences, hardships, or specific callings. Whatever the means, staying spiritually aligned with God is crucial to understanding and stepping into the destiny He has designed for you.

To fulfill your destiny, you must surrender your will to God. Surrender is not a one-time event but a daily commitment to trust God's plans over your own.

"Father, if you are willing, take this cup from me; yet not my will, but yours be done" (Luke 22:42, NIV).

This prayer of surrender shows the importance of yielding to God's will, even when it may be challenging or contrary to our desires. In moments of uncertainty or difficulty, surrender allows you to trust that God's way is always better and that He is working all things together for your good (*Romans 8:28, NIV*).

Surrendering to God involves letting go of control and trusting Him to guide you into your destiny. Obedience is a vital part of spiritual alignment. To fulfill your destiny, you must be willing to follow God's instructions, even when they don't make sense or when they require sacrifice.

The Bible provides examples of people who fulfilled their destinies because they obeyed God, such as Abraham, Moses, and David. *"If you are willing and obedient, you will eat the good things of the land"* (Isaiah 1:19, NIV). Fulfilling your destiny requires excellent faith.

God's plans for you often go beyond what you can understand or imagine. Faith is trusting God even when the path is unclear.

"And without faith, it is impossible to please God because anyone who comes to Him must believe that He exists and that He rewards those who earnestly seek Him" (Hebrews 11:6, NIV).

When you are spiritually aligned, your faith grows as you trust God's promises and character. Like Joseph in the Bible, who endured years of hardship before fulfilling his destiny as a leader in Egypt, you may face obstacles. Still, faith enables you to persevere and continue believing that God will bring His plan for your life to pass.

Distractions and hindrances can pull you away from fulfilling your destiny. These can take the form of temptations, unhealthy relationships, or even personal ambitions that are not in accordance with God's will.

Spiritual alignment involves staying focused on God's purposes and being aware of anything that may lead you off course.

"Throw off everything that hinders and the sin that so easily entangles. And let us run with perseverance the race marked out for us" (Hebrews 12:1, NIV).

As you pursue your destiny, there will be moments when you feel weak or discouraged. In these times, you must rely on God's strength and grace.

"My grace is sufficient for you, for my power is made perfect in weakness" (2 Corinthians 12:9, NIV).

God's grace empowers you to keep moving forward, even when the journey gets tough. Spiritual alignment involves recognizing that you cannot fulfill your destiny in your strength. You need God's empowerment through His spirit to accomplish the great things He has called you to do.

"I can do all this through Him who gives me strength" (Philippians 4:13, NIV).

Maintaining a close, ongoing relationship with God is vital to fulfilling your destiny. Prayer, worship, and spending time in His Word are essential to aligning with Him.

"I am the vine; you are the branches. If you remain in me and I in you, you will bear much fruit; apart from me, you can do nothing" (John

15:5, NIV).

By staying connected to God through daily communion, you receive the guidance, strength, and wisdom needed to continue walking in your destiny.

Without this close relationship, it's easy to become disconnected and miss the fullness of God's plans.

Fulfilling your destiny is about achieving earthly success and living with an eternal perspective. God's Kingdom is eternal, and when your life is aligned with His Kingdom's purposes, your actions have a lasting impact beyond this world.

"Seek first the Kingdom of God and His righteousness" (Matthew 6:33, NIV) encourages us, knowing that everything else will fall into place when we prioritize God's Kingdom.

Walking in spiritual alignment means living with the awareness that your life is part of something bigger than yourself.

You are part of God's grand plan to bring His Kingdom to earth, and your obedience to His calling plays a significant role in His eternal purposes.

When you fulfill your destiny through spiritual alignment, you leave behind a legacy of faith that impacts future generations.

Like the heroes of faith mentioned in Hebrews 11, your life can inspire others to pursue their God-given purpose and trust in His faithfulness.

Fulfilling your destiny is about more than what you accomplish in this life; it is also about the spiritual legacy you leave behind. Your obedience, faith, and alignment with God's will influence those around you and can impact your family, community, and beyond.

How to Stay Aligned with God's Kingdom Plan

Staying aligned with God's Kingdom plan is essential for fulfilling your purpose and living a life that honors Him. It involves being intentional about your relationship with God, understanding His will, and making choices that reflect His values and priorities.

To align with God's Kingdom plan, you must first have a personal relationship with Him. This begins with accepting Jesus Christ as your Lord and Savior.

"For God so loved the world that he gave his one and only Son, that whoever believes in him shall not perish but have eternal life" (John 3:16, NIV).

Understanding and following God's will is crucial for aligning with His Kingdom plan.

"Trust in the Lord with all your heart and lean not on your understanding; in all your ways submit to Him, and He will make your paths straight" (Proverbs 3:5-6, NIV).

Pray for wisdom and discernment in your decisions. The Holy Spirit guides and empowers you to make choices that align with God's Kingdom.

Be attentive to His promptings and leading in your daily life. Ensure that your personal goals reflect His priorities to stay aligned with God's kingdom plan. Your ambitions should be rooted in what glorifies God and advances His Kingdom.

Assess your goals and ensure they align with God's purposes. This may include goals related to serving others, sharing the Gospel, and growing your faith.

Reflect on your motives behind your goals. Are they self-centered or focused on bringing glory to God?

"Work at it with all your heart, as working for the Lord, not for human masters" (Colossians 3:23, NIV).

Living according to God's values is critical to aligning with His Kingdom plan. This means embodying the principles found in the Bible and reflecting Christ's character in your life. Jesus taught us to love one another. Show kindness and compassion to those around you, reflecting the love of Christ.

"We love because he first loved us" (1 John 4:19, NIV).

Stay humble and recognize that all you have comes from God.

"Do nothing out of selfish ambition or vain conceit. Rather, in humility, value others above yourselves" (Philippians 2:3, NIV).

Continual spiritual growth is vital for staying aligned with God's Kingdom plan. This involves actively seeking to know God more and becoming more like Him. Invest time in learning and growing in your faith. This can include reading books, attending workshops, or listening to sermons that challenge and inspire you.

Reflect on Your Progress:

Take time to reflect on your spiritual journey. Consider how far you've come and what areas you need to grow.

"Grow in the grace and knowledge of our Lord and Savior Jesus Christ" (2 Peter 3:18, NIV).

God has a unique calling for each person. Staying aligned with His Kingdom plan requires you to focus on His specific purpose for your life.

Discover the gifts and talents God has given you and use them for His glory.

"Each of you should use whatever gift you have received to serve others, as faithful stewards of God's grace in its various forms" (1 Peter 4:10, NIV).

Understand that challenges may arise, but remain committed to your calling.

"Therefore, my dear brothers and sisters, stand firm. Let nothing move you. Always give yourselves fully to the work of the Lord, because you know that your labor in the Lord is not in vain" (1 Corinthians 15:58, NIV).

Staying aligned with God's Kingdom plan requires patience and trust in His timing. God's plans may unfold differently than you expect, but His timing is perfect.

Understand that growth and change take time.

"Wait for the Lord; be strong and take heart and wait for the Lord" (Psalm 27:14, NIV).

Remember that God is in control of all circumstances. Trust that He knows what is best for you and works everything together for your good.

"And we know that in all things God works for the good of those who love him, who have been called according to his purpose" (Romans 8:28, NIV).

Living out God's Kingdom plan involves serving others. Serving is a tangible way to express God's love and advance His Kingdom. Find opportunities to serve in your church or community.

This can include volunteering, mentoring, or participating in outreach programs that meet the needs of others. Be generous with your time, talents, and resources.

"Each of you should give what you have decided in your heart to give, not reluctantly or under compulsion, for God loves a cheerful giver" (2 Corinthians 9:7, NIV).

Staying aligned with God's Kingdom plan requires focusing on eternity. Life on earth is temporary, but our choices have eternal significance. Make choices that reflect your eternal values and priorities. This means investing in relationships, sharing the Gospel, and living a life that points others to Christ.

Remember that your efforts in God's Kingdom will have lasting rewards. Matthew 6:19-21 reminds us not to store up treasures on earth but to focus on treasures in heaven.

Unlocking God's Blessings Through Obedience and Focus

God desires to bless His children, but there are keys to unlocking those blessings. One of the most significant keys is obedience.

When we obey God and remain focused on His will, we open the door to His blessings. To grasp the importance of obedience and focus, we must first understand who God is. God is good, loving, and just. His plans for us are always for our good.

Believing God wants what is best for us encourages us to obey Him. Obedience to God is not just about following rules; it's about trusting Him and His wisdom.

"If you love me, keep my commands" (John 14:15, NIV).

This verse highlights that our obedience reflects our love for God. The Bible is filled with instructions on how to live a life that pleases God.

When we study and apply God's Word, we align our lives with His will. God speaks to us through prayer, Scripture, and the Holy Spirit. When attentive to His guidance, we can follow His will more closely.

Focus is essential in our walk with God. It helps us prioritize our lives and focus on what truly matters.

Identify what God wants for your life. Setting goals that align with His will helps you stay focused on your spiritual journey. Life is full of distractions that can lead us away from God's purpose.

By focusing on His Kingdom and ignoring distractions, we create space for God's blessings. Obedience unlocks God's blessings in our lives.

"If you fully obey the Lord your God and carefully follow all his commands... all these blessings will come on you and accompany you" (Deuteronomy 28:1-2, NIV).

God promises to bless us materially as we obey Him. This can include provision, stability, and success in our endeavors. Obedience leads to a deeper relationship with God, resulting in spiritual growth and fulfillment.

"The one who looks into the perfect law, the law of liberty, and

perseveres, being no hearer who forgets but a doer who acts, he will be blessed in his doing" (James 1:25, ESV).

When we are obedient and focused on God, we experience the peace and joy that come from living in harmony with His will. Obedience brings a sense of peace. Knowing we are walking in God's ways alleviates anxiety and uncertainty.

Following God's path allows us to experience joy, even amid challenges.

"Rejoice in the Lord always. I will repeat it: Rejoice!" (Philippians 4:4, NIV).

Abraham obeyed God's call to leave his homeland, and God blessed him abundantly.

Moses led the Israelites out of Egypt by obeying God's commands, and God blessed them with freedom and guidance. Jesus demonstrated perfect obedience to the Father, and through His sacrifice, He unlocked salvation and blessings for all who believe.

When you commit to obedience and focus, you will see the fruit of your efforts. As you obey God and remain focused, you will grow in understanding His ways.

Obedience leads to transformation. You will start to see changes in your character, attitudes, and actions. God rewards obedience with blessings that may come in various forms, including peace, joy, provision, and opportunities.

CONCLUSION

The Lasting Legacy Of A Focused Life

Focus impacts every part of our lives—our spiritual growth, relationships, work, and personal goals. When we focus on God, He directs our paths and helps us live a life that is balanced, meaningful, and full of His peace.

We've learned the importance of prioritizing time with God in our spiritual lives. Focus allows us to build deep, meaningful connections with others in our relationships. When we give people our full attention and show them the love of Christ, we strengthen our bonds and positively impact the lives of those around us.

A focused life helps us love and serve others as God calls us. It also allows us to be productive and efficient at work or in our personal goals. We find success and fulfillment when we commit our work to God and focus on doing it for His glory.

A life of focus also helps us make wise decisions, manage our time effectively, and use our talents to honor God. When we stay focused on God, we guard our hearts and minds against things that distract us.

By filling our minds with good and godly things, we protect ourselves from distractions that can steal our time and energy.

A focused life is also a life of intentionality. It means we deliberate how we spend our time and what we focus on each day. Living with intentionality means making the most of every opportunity to grow, serve, and fulfill God's purpose for our lives.

When we live purposefully, we are no longer aimlessly drifting through life. Instead, we are anchored in God's plan for us, confident that He guides us every step of the way.

By trusting God and focusing on His will, we walk a path of purpose, and every step we take moves us closer to His plans for us. Living a focused life doesn't just help us accomplish our goals or avoid distractions; it leads us to the fullness of life God has promised.

A focused life is fulfilling in which we experience the joy, peace, and contentment that comes from walking in God's will.

It's a life in which we feel satisfied knowing that we are making the most of the gifts and opportunities God has given us. The ultimate reward of living a focused life is hearing God's words.

"Commit your way to the Lord; trust in Him, and He will do this" (Psalm 37:5, NIV).

A focused life benefits the individual living it and profoundly impacts future generations. The choices we make, the values we live by, and the example we set leave a lasting legacy for those who come after us.

Living a focused, purpose-driven life, we plant seeds to build a strong foundation for our children, grandchildren, and the wider community.

Every life has influence, whether we realize it or not. The way we live, the decisions we make, and the priorities we hold dear speak volumes to those around us, especially the younger generation.

When we live a focused life, driven by purpose and aligned with God's will, we create a model for others to aspire to. A concentrated life also helps to create a legacy of integrity and character. When we make decisions based on godly principles, we build a reputation of honesty, integrity, and faithfulness.

Living with integrity sets a powerful example for the younger generation, showing them the importance of standing firm in their values, even when it's complicated.

Our focus on doing what is right, even when no one is watching, teaches others the value of living with moral conviction. God often blesses not only the individual who is faithful but also their descendants.

The Bible shows examples of generational blessings from living a focused, faithful life. One such example is Abraham. God made a covenant with Abraham that extended to his descendants because of his faith and obedience.

"I will make you into a great nation, and I will bless you; I will make your name great, and you will be a blessing" (Genesis 12:2, NIV).

A focused life also strengthens families and communities. When we prioritize our relationship with God and live according to His purpose, we create a ripple effect that influences our family and community.

A focused life centered on God helps to build a robust and stable foundation for future generations. Parents who live with focus and purpose raise children who are more likely to develop strong moral and spiritual foundations. These children, in turn, become adults who contribute positively to society and pass on those values to their children.

Living a focused life helps to break the cycles of distraction, aimlessness, and confusion that can often plague families and communities. Without focus, people can drift through life, constantly reacting to circumstances rather than proactively pursuing God's purpose.

This lack of direction can lead to negative consequences such as poor decision-making, unhealthy relationships, and spiritual stagnation. Living purposefully shows future generations that life is not meant to be lived aimlessly but with intentionality.

We demonstrate that a focused life, rooted in God's will, brings fulfillment, peace, and success. Our example teaches others that they can, too, break free from the world's distractions and live a life of purpose, focused on what truly matters.

Living a focused life encourages future generations to seek God's plan for themselves. It teaches them that true success and fulfillment come from aligning their lives with God's purpose.

When we live a life focused on God, we inspire future generations to do the same. They see the fruit of a life with purpose—peace, joy, contentment, and spiritual fulfillment—and are encouraged to seek God's will for their lives.

Our focused lives become a powerful testimony to God's goodness and faithfulness, motivating others to trust Him with their journeys. As you move forward, keep your eyes fixed on Jesus, trust His guidance, and live with purpose and focus.

No matter where you are in your journey, it's never too late to start living a focused life that honors God. And remember, with God's help, you can achieve great things and fulfill the unique purpose He has for you.

Let *"Commit your way to the Lord; trust in Him, and He will do this"* (Psalm 37:5, NIV) be your guide. Now, go forth confidently, knowing that God is with you every step of the way as you live a life of focus, purpose, and joy.

A SPECIAL CALL TO SALVATION & NEW BEGINNINGS FROM APOSTLE DR. DAVID PHILEMON

Dear Beloved,

God loves you deeply and has brought you to this moment for a reason. No matter your past, His love and forgiveness are available to you.

The Bible says in John 3:16, "For God so loved the world that He gave His one and only Son, that whoever believes in Him shall not perish but have eternal life." Jesus Christ came to save you, offering you a new life of purpose and peace.

If you're ready to accept Jesus as your Lord and Savior, pray this simple prayer:

The Salvation Prayer

"Heavenly Father, I come to You in the Name of Jesus. I acknowledge that I am a sinner in need of a Savior. I believe that Jesus Christ is Your Son, that He died for my sins, and that You raised Him from the dead. I repent of my sins and turn to You with my

Whole heart. Jesus, I ask You to come into my life. Be my Lord and my Savior. I surrender my life to You. Fill me with Your Holy Spirit, guide me on the path of righteousness, and help me to follow Your script for my life. Thank you, Father, for saving me. In the name of Jesus. Amen."

Welcome to the Family of God!

If you have just prayed this prayer, Congratulations! You are now a child of God, and heaven is rejoicing. Your journey has begun, and we're here to support you as you grow in faith and discover God's unique plans for you.

Next Steps:
• Connect with a Bible-believing church.
• Read the Bible Daily: God's Word is your guide.
• Pray Regularly: Prayer is your lifeline to God.
• Share Your Faith: Don't keep the good news to yourself.

www.ingramcontent.com/pod-product-compliance
Lightning Source LLC
Chambersburg PA
CBHW060445040426
42331CB00044B/2625